The
LEARNINGS
OF A
LIFETIME

Jim Imes

Order this book online at www.trafford.com
or email orders@trafford.com

Most Trafford titles are also available at major online book retailers.

Printed in the United States of America.

ISBN: 978-1-4669-7961-1 (sc)
ISBN: 978-1-4669-7960-4 (e)

Trafford rev. 05/07/2013

 www.trafford.com

North America & international
toll-free: 1 888 232 4444 (USA & Canada)
phone: 250 383 6864 ✦ fax: 812 355 4082

Contents

Dedication

This book is dedicated to every single person in my life that has made me the person I am today! I will name and credit as many as I can remember.

I want to give special thanks to Carla Ann Imes for help me edit and proof read my book.

My Mother: Rita Imes

My Dad: James Verle Imes

My Grandfather: Verle Clair Imes

My Grandmother: Florence Imes

My Young Brother: Bob Imes

My Youngest Brother: Bruce E. Imes

My Uncle Bruce Imes

My Uncle Kenny Imes

My Aunt Myrtle Pigg

My Uncle Donald Pigg

My First Wife Theresa Gayle Waldren

My Son: Chad Anthony Imes

My Son: Ryan James Imes

My Mother-in-Law: Afton Waldren

My Father-in-law: Father: Bob Waldren

My 2nd Wife Carla Ann Imes

My Stepdaughter Janel Brannon

My Stepson Gregory Brannon

My Daughter-in-Law: Erin Brannon

My Granddaughters: Ella and Megyn Brannon

My Granddaughter Dylan Harrison

My Great Grandson Dominic Brannon Huerta

My Son-in-Law: George Harrison

All my teachers, especially my Catholic teachers

All my coaches

All my friends

All my fellow employees and the Dealership Owners I worked for

Chapter 1

PREFACE

This book was written to help people. Even though the first chapter has a lot of religious content in it, this book is not all about religion. I believe in God but there is so much more I truly believe that will benefit all people.

THE LEARNING'S OF A LIFETIME
EXPLANATIONS OF UNIVERSALS LAWS,
RELIGIOUS LAWS, LIFE'S LEARNING LESSONS &
WORK RELATED WISDOM
(AND I'M STILL LEARNING EVERYDAY)

Take every sentence and paragraph, stop, and reflect on it before you move to the next. If you read the whole composite and don't do this, you will likely not retain or remember 90% of it. Study it. When you reflect, ask yourself, what is the message? (Lesson of life, lesson of business, lesson of values and morals), what is this person trying to convey to the reader. Then you will retain it, pass it on, and hopefully use it for a Lifetime!

Religious Knowledge that affects everyone's everyday life:

- You cannot live life to the fullest unless you know the rules. Life is that of giving and receiving.
- "Whatsoever a man soweth that shall he will also reap." This means that whatever man sends out in will return to him; what he gives, he will receive. (The main rule is that Man/Woman must give without expecting anything in return.) The giving must be unselfish. If you are giving because you want or expect something in return, then it will not happen. Also the return will come as more than expected, and not necessarily from the same source. Some say as much as 10 times more! Another way of saying this is, "What you reap is what you sow." What you put out comes back to you. In other words, everyone will experience the consequences of his own acts. If his acts are right, he will receive good consequences: if they are not, he will suffer for it.
- If man gives hate, he will receive hate; if he gives love, he will receive love; if he gives criticism, he will receive criticism; if he lies he will be lied to; if he cheats he will be cheated; if he doesn't forgive then he will not be forgiven. And you must know that these will happen to you but not necessarily from the same person.

- A person with an imaging faculty trained to image only good brings good into his life, every righteous desire of the heart: he will have health, wealth, love, friends, perfect self-expression, and his highest ideals, (values).

A Lesson on How the Subconscious Mind Works

The subconscious mind has no sense of humor. The subconscious is somewhat like a computer. What you punch on the keyboard or upload is what will happen. If you tell yourself I can't, and then your subconscious says, ok you can't. If you allow your conscious mind to think negative, then your subconscious has no choice but to agree and make it happen, and it does it with amazing accuracy!

Examples of How Your Conscious and Subconscious Mind Communicates

1. Conscious: "You're scaring me to death!"
   Subconscious: Ok I'll keep scaring you.
2. Conscious: "Big boys don't cry." (This is an old, common, and very bad program)
   Subconscious: Ok I won't let you cry even when you're happy or sad.
3. Conscious: "I can never hit bull's eye in darts."
   Subconscious: Ok (I will do everything in my power to see that you can't hit a bull's eye in darts).

4   Conscious: "Hey Steve. You're killing me, Ha!" (This is not a funny saying but a lot of people use it)

5   Subconscious: Ok (I will kill you a little bit at a time)

6   Conscious: "If that ever happened to me I would take a gun and shoot myself". (A friend of mine always said this and he committed suicide with a gun).
     Subconscious: Ok let's get your gun and kill you.

7   Conscious: "Man, am I ever stupid." (Is that anyway to talk to yourself?)
     Subconscious: Ok I'll keep you stupid.

8   Conscious: This headache is killing me.

9   Subconscious: Ok I will make it hurt as much as I can.

Take the time now to see how many you can think of. Now change them to a positive thought.

Some Great Thought Related Sayings:
Think About It!

So you see that every thought and everything you say has either a negative or a positive effect on you. Why? Because your subconscious doesn't think on its own, it just processes what it is told by the conscious mind. And I'll say it again. It does this with amazing accuracy.

We know now, from a scientific standpoint, that death could be overcome by stamping the subconscious mind with the conviction of eternal youth and eternal life. Why? Because the subconscious being simply power without direction, carries out orders without questioning that the conscious mind feeds it. The human body was originally made to last about 120 years! In recent news a lady lived to be 122 years old. There have been cases in history where people in the Bible have lived to be 130, thou there is no real proof.

- People can alter their lives by altering their attitudes.
- What the mind can conceive and believe, the mind can achieve.
- By man's word and thoughts he starts into action unseen forces and can rebuild his body or remold his life.
- It is often wiser to _replace_ the bad programs in life, before learning new programs.
- The conscious mind sees life, as it appears to be. It sees death, disaster, sickness, poverty, and limitations of every kind, and it impresses the subconscious mind. It is because of this that you need to take control of what you think and say. The conscious mind gives orders to your subconscious mind. This is the place that you are to fill and no one else can fill. Something you are to do, which no one else can do. This is where dreams are built and fulfilled.

How the Super Subconscious works!

The super subconscious mind is the God Mind within each person. It is the realm of perfect ideas.

I believe (My personal opinion), that the Super Subconscious is the place where God lives. A lot of people agree or think he resides in our hearts. It is the place some people touch when they are in the zone or when you're instinct takes over. It is where your own personal heaven is. It is where your instinct exists.

I believe that all people at one time or another have had a situation (such as a near automobile accident for example), and things happened so fast that when it was over you can't possibly imagine how you reacted so fast and so rightly. You know your conscious couldn't possibly think-react, think-react, think-react that fast and with that much accuracy. Your perfect super subconscious took over for you. So you see that by knowing it exists and how it works you need to make sure you program it correctly. He is saying the kingdom is within man. <Jim Imes>

Sickness-Unhappiness-Fear-Worry

The man who sends out only good will to his fellow man, and who is without fear, cannot be touched or influenced by the negative thoughts of others.

- Tell yourself, "I am fully equipped for the divine plan of my life, and I am fearless in grasping opportunities".
- Bless your enemy and you rob him of his ammunition.
- So long as a person resists a situation, they will have it with them. If they run away from it, it will run after them like a lion.
- Continually making believe impresses the subconscious, (just think of small children.) If one makes believe he is rich, and makes believe he is successful, in due time he will reap. Children are great at make believe, they have such great imaginations.

Having a great imagination is what dreams are made of. Having a great imagination is what led to all the great inventions we enjoy. In some cases a great imagination and curiosity is greater than intelligence. Jim Imes

Fear is Lack of Faith.

- Perfect love casts out fear, he that fears is not made perfect in love, and love is the fulfillment of life.
- How can I get rid of fear? By walking up to the thing you are afraid of. The lion takes its fierceness from your fear. Walk up to the lion, and he will disappear. Run away and the lion runs after you.
- Man can only vanquish fear by walking up to the thing he is afraid of. Remember the lion.

Face the lion because his strength is feeding off of your fear.

- Desire is a tremendous force, and must be directed in the right channels, or chaos ensues. Man/Woman should always demand only that which is theirs by divine right.
- *Christianity is founded upon the law of forgiveness.*
- If a person desires riches, they must be rich first in consciousness. If you wish to be rich, you must be <u>organized</u>. All people with great wealth are orderly and order is heaven's first law.
- Many people are in ignorance of the fact that gifts and things are investments, and that hoarding and saving invariably leads to loss.
- God's retirement plan is out of this world.
- The Ten Commandments are not multiple choices.
- God's last name is not "Dammit".
- Man's supply is inexhaustible and unfailing when fully trusted, but faith or trust must precede the demonstration.
- Faith is the substance of things hoped for. Faith holds the vision steady, and the adverse pictures are dissolved.
- The Bible states that the battle is God's, not mans and that man is always to stand still and see the salvation of the Lord. This indicates that the super subconscious mind (or the Christ within) is the department that fights man's battles and relieves him

of burdens. Therefore man violates this law if he carries a burden, and a burden is an adverse thought or condition. And this thought or condition is rooted in the subconscious.

The words hate and love are two of the most powerful words in the English language!

The English language is the foulest language in the world as far as cussing goes. No other language in use even comes close.

The subconscious is often impressed through music. Music has a fourth dimensional quality and releases the soul from imprisonment. It makes wonderful things seem possible, and makes accomplishments a lot easier! I know an ex-professional baseball pitcher that listened to music and relaxed before the game instead of over thinking or worrying about the game. It worked for him and it can work for you. (Jim Imes)

In the twinkling of an eye, man's release will come when he realizes there is no power in evil.

The subconscious must be impressed with the truth that God is the giver and He is the gift; therefore as God is one with the giver, He is one with the gift.

Real love is selfless and free from fear. It pours itself out upon the object of its affection without demanding any return. Its joy is in the joy of giving.

Love is God in manifestation, and the strongest magnetic force in the universe. Pure, unselfish love draws to itself. It does not need to seek or demand.

Scarcely anyone has the faintest conception of real love. Man is selfish, tyrannical, or fearful in his affections, thereby losing the thing he loves.

Jealousy is the worst enemy of love, for your imagination will run amuck. Seeing your loved one attracted to another, and invariably these fears will manifest if they are not neutralized. You can never receive what you have never given. Give a perfect love and you will receive a perfect love.

No man is your enemy, no man is your friend, and every man is your teacher. So one should become impersonal and learn what each man has to teach him, and soon he will learn his lessons and be free.

- If you are going the wrong direction, remember, God allows U-turns.
- All disease, all unhappiness, come from the violation of the law of love. Man's hate, resentment and criticism, come back to laden him with sickness and sorrow.
- If you cannot right a wrong then doing something of kindness in the present can neutralize its effect.
- Know that God is your supply for every demand, and that His spoken word releases this supply.

- Ask whatever you want in the name of Jesus Christ and you will receive if it is your divine right.
- Draw near to God and He will draw near to you.
- Speak the Word to God and then do nothing until you get a definite lead.
- Intuition is a spiritual faculty and does not explain, but simply points the way.

The science of numbers and the readings of horoscopes, keep man down on the mental, (or mortal) plane, for they deal only with the Karmic path. Now I like to read my Horoscope every day, not because I believe that one Horoscope fits everyone in the world, but because they usually have a positive statement or idea that can prompt me to do something positive or good that day that I normally wouldn't think of.

- The Bible is a book dealing with the science of the mind. It is a book telling man how to release his soul (subconscious mind) from bondage.
- It is impossible for man to release more than he thinks is possible, for man is bound by the limited expectancies of the subconscious. He must enlarge his expectancies is order to receive in a larger way.
- Man should demand enormous sums of money, which are his by divine right, reach Him under grace, in perfect ways. Just ask for it divinely in the name of Jesus Christ.

Father I take nothing less than I've asked for, but more!

- I desire only that which God desires for me.

What Are Affirmations?

Affirmations are spoken statements used to achieve a desired state. They are always stated in the present, always positive, and always stated as if it has already happened in your life.

Why Use Affirmations?

Using affirmations neutralizes and replaces negative subconscious beliefs. Even if you have trouble controlling your thoughts, you can control your words.

Repeating an affirmation over and over impresses the subconscious and gradually replaces former beliefs with new, positive ones.

Affirmations work best when they are absolutely satisfying to your consciousness. Feel it. Believe in your power to be.

Affirmation to Rid Yourself of Resentment

I cast this burden of resentment on the Christ within, and I go free, to be loving, harmonious, and happy forever and ever in the name of Jesus Christ, Amen.

Affirmation to Show the Way

Infinite Spirit, reveal to me the way. Open the door and let me know if there is anything for me to do.

Affirmation for Abundance

Infinite Spirit, open the way for my immediate supply, let all that is mine by divine right now reach me in great avalanches of abundance in the name of Jesus Christ, Amen.

Affirmation for Talent

Infinite Spirit, give me a definite lead, reveal to me my perfect self-expression, show me which talent I am to make use of now, in the name of Jesus Christ, Amen.

Affirmation for the Divine Selection

Infinite Spirit, open the way for my right home, my right friend, my right position, my right soul mate. I give thanks it now manifests under grace in a perfect way.

Affirmation for Money

I cast this burden of lack on the Christ within and I go free to have plenty of wealth.

Affirmation to Rid Yourself of Disease

I deny this appearance of disease. It is unreal, therefore it cannot register in my subconscious; I am in perfect health in the divine mind.

Affirmation for Work or Business

I have a wonderful work, in a wonderful way; I give wonderful service, for wonderful pay; or I have a wonderful business, in a wonderful way; I give a wonderful service, for wonderful pay.

Daily Affirmation for the New Day

Say this every morning upon waking. "Your will, will be done my Lord this day! I give thanks for this perfect day, and miracle shall follow miracle and wonders shall never cease."

Affirmation for Another's Wealth

Infinite spirit open the way for great abundance for _____. He/She is an irresistible magnet for all that belongs to him/her by divine right.

Affirmation for Prosperity

God is my unfailing supply, and large sums of money come to me quickly, under grace, in perfect ways in the name of Jesus Christ our Lord, Amen.

Affirmation for Health

Divine love floods my consciousness with health, and every cell in my body is filled with light and heals every molecule of my body, in the name of Jesus Christ our Lord, Amen.

Affirmation for the Eyesight

My eyes are God's eyes, I see with the eyes of the Spirit. I see clearly, in the name of Jesus Christ our Lord, Amen.

Affirmation for the Hearing

My ears are God's ears, I hear with the ears of the spirit.

Affirmation for Freedom From all Burdens

I cast this burden of _____on the Christ within, and I go free.

Affirmation for Everyone

I am now healthy, wealthy, and wise. I am a great saver and a great investor, forever and ever in the name of Jesus Christ, Amen.

Believe and dream and put it in the hands of God.

I may not be perfect but Jesus thinks I am to die for.

Write Your Own Affirmations

Write your own affirmations or borrow some and hang them on your bathroom mirror and read them several times each and every day while you are shaving, brushing your teeth, or putting on your makeup. You will be reprogramming your mind, and you will be amazed at how many come true!

Chapter 2

WISDOM AND COMMON SENSE

You don't have to brush all of your teeth, only the ones you want to keep.

I tried but it didn't work is a lot better than *I wish I'd tried.*

It is especially hard to work for money you've already spent for something you didn't need. (Could be talking about credit cards?)

About gossip: If you didn't hear it with your own ears or see it with you own eyes, then don't invent it with your small mind or share it with your big mouth. Gossip is one of the most destructive and negative things you can do in business and life. Jim Imes

Apologizing does not always mean you are wrong and the other person is right. It merely means that you value your relationship with them more than your ego.

Did you know that when you envy someone, it's because you really like that person?

Some people have enough money for the rest of their life, (unless they buy something.)

Usually when you're young, you know everything . . . except how to make a living.

When you're a teenager your parents seem very dumb and you know everything. It's amazing how smart they get in a few years. You think they must have gone to college. There is a scientific reason for teens thinking this way. The frontal lobes, responsible for reasoning and problem solving, develop last, usually in the early twenties.

Money isn't everything, but it sure keeps you in touch with your kids.

If someone betrays you once, it's his fault; if he betrays you twice, it's your fault.

"How many times have you taken action on things you don't desire? Imagine if you took action on the things you do desire."

Great minds discuss ideas; average minds discuss events; small minds discuss people, (gossip).

If you think too much about what other people think about you. You will always be their prisoner.

Maybe it's not always trying to fix something that is broken. Maybe it's about starting over and creating something better.

There comes a time in life when you have to let go of all of the pointless drama and the people that create it and surround yourself with the people that make you happy and make you laugh. Life is too short to be anything but happy! Some people are all about drama. They especially get so dramatic when they get mad. Jim Imes

Something might be more important than the truth; but right now I can't think of any.

You need to protect a family members mine just like you protect their body!

Bits of Wisdom

Live beneath your means and within your seams.

Return everything you borrow.

Give all the clothes you haven't worn in the last year to charity. This is how you can determine what clothes to donate. Hang all your clothes with all the hangers facing the same direction. As you wear and wash your clothes then hang your clothes with the hanger in the opposite direction. Wait a year and go through all four seasons. If you still have clothes facing the original direction, then donate them. Jim Imes

Every day: take a 30-minute walk in your neighborhood.

Strive for excellence, not perfection. Jim Imes

Take time to be alone.

Plastic bread tabs and a permanent mark make it great for tagging the cords to your electronic equipment so that if you move you don't have to get out the manual and refigure where each cord goes.

If you don't know how to do something, you can't learn any younger than right now.

If you can't get a job in America then don't move to another country.

Reread a favorite book.

He, who loses money, loses much; he, who loses a friend, loses more; he who loses faith, loses all. If you are lucky enough to have 5 really close friends, (these are the ones that keep in contact with you and show up to your funeral), then you have been blessed. Jim Imes

Beautiful young people are acts of nature, but beautiful old people are works of art. You can go to a Veterans Center; Rehab Hospital; VFW, (Veterans of Foreign Wars), etc. and meet and talk to some of the wisest, most interesting people, with the greatest stories. Jim Imes

The heart is wiser than the intellect.

Guilt: If you feel guilt when you do something then that is your instinct; values; morals; or perhaps something that is against the law; and it's telling you that you probably shouldn't be doing it. Jim Imes

Fortune truly helps those who are of good judgment.

Speak only well of people and you need never whisper.

It is better to share happiness than keep it to yourself.

Be direct; usually one can accomplish more that way.

For every 60 seconds of anger, you lose one minute of happiness.

Kindness: a language the deaf can hear, the blind can see, and the mute can speak.

When you see someone without a smile, give him one of yours.

The days are very long, but the years are very short. In a blink of the eyes your children are grown up; you've gone from a young person to a senior, etc. That's why it's so important to live each day as if it's your last. Jim Imes

Respect cost nothing but so many people lack it. Jim Imes

Happiness is not too hard to find, it's how you treat it once you get hold of it that counts.

Sorrow looks back, worry looks around, and faith looks up. If you live or dwell on bad things in the past it causes worry and depression. If you worry or dwell on the future it causes anxiety. It's been proven that 95% of future worries never come to past. Always live your life in the present. Jim Imes

When one door of happiness closes another opens: but often we look so long at the closed door that we do not see the one which has been opened for us.

Insanity is inherited. You get it from your children.

Insanity is doing the wrong or same thing over and over and expecting difference results.

Children should be given only a modest and sensible allowance, and they should save up for things. I was raised this way and our children were too. It sure came in handy later in their lives.

Pre pay for your burial expenses; funeral; casket; head stone; plot; etc. It gives comfort to your family to know you chose what you wanted. It's not the responsibility of your family to pay and plan for your burial. Jim Imes

Never allow your child to call you by your first name; they haven't known you long enough. Out of respect it should be something like; Mom, dad, father, mother, Mommy, daddy, etc. In cases where they introduce you to someone they should say something like, "this is my dad Jim, or my Mom Rita." Jim Imes

No dream is too high for those with their eyes in the sky.

To acquire knowledge, one must study: but to acquire wisdom, one must observe.

Listen twice as much as you talk. God gave you two ears and one mouth for a reason. You can learn more by being a good listener.

Do what you can to show you care about other people, and you will make our world a better place.

Dumping sadness on another person is a selfish act. Ask if you can vent to a family member or a friend if they approve, or go see a therapist to vent or solve a problem.

Some people can't say no to anyone or anything. We all know these types of people.

Their hearts are bigger than their common sense or their pocket books. Jim Imes

Humility is the mother of all virtues, courage the father, integrity the child, and wisdom the grandchild.

Excellence I can reach for, perfection is God's business.

Love what you do. Believe in your instincts, and you'd better be able to pick yourself up and brush yourself off every day.

Take time to smell the roses. Go outside and sit or look around and praise God for such a beautiful day. Listen to the birds; feel the sunshine; smell the air; give thanks that you are able to do these things. This will relax you and also make you appreciate life. Jim Imes

If you count your blessings you can't help but feel great. Jim Imes

Embrace everyday miracles.

Never deprive someone of hope; it may be all they have.

Commit random acts of kindness and senseless beauty.

To get what you want out of life first decide what you want. Then set up a plan and goals to attain them. Jim Imes

Discovery consists of seeing what everybody has seen, and thinking what nobody has thought.

Wisdom is knowledge rightly applied. For example: teaching children about hot and cold.

Success: if you have tried to do something and failed, you are vastly better off than if you had tried to do nothing and succeeded.

Friendship: never explain: your friends do not need it, and your enemies will not believe it anyway.

Everybody gets nervous before a performance. The secret is to get the butterflies in your stomach to fly in formation.

Be a fountain, not a drain and don't be a _whipping post_ or doormat for everyone else's problems. Jim Imes

You can learn more about a person by playing a round of golf with them or by going to dinner with them and observing how they treat a waiter or waitress. Jim Imes

Progress always involves risk: you can't steal second base and keep your foot on first base.

All things are difficult before they are easy.

One of the greatest mistakes a man can make is to be afraid of making one.

Some things are more painful than the truth, but right now, I can't think of any.

It's better to look ahead and prepare, than to look back and regret.

You can prepare for the future by planning and saving for emergencies; retirement; a new vehicle, etc. or you can spend every penny you have now; borrow beyond your limits; have every toy or everything the Jones have; and live a life of misery and poverty when you get old. Live for today but plan like you are going to live forever. In other words you can play today and pay tomorrow, or you can pay today and play tomorrow. Jim Imes

Kindness is the ability to love people more than they deserve.

You can't turn back the clock, but you can wind it up again.

If you have joy in your heart, it will be known by the look on your face.

Honesty is the first chapter in the book of wisdom.

Nobody fails if they have given their best effort.

Don't be afraid to take a big step. You can't cross a 6-foot hole with 2 three-foot steps.

Don't try to be anything but what you are. But make sure you do that perfectly.

Tact is the ability to describe others as they see themselves.

You cannot adjust the wind, but you can adjust the sails.

Don't wait for your ship to come in: swim out to it.

Some people die at the age of 30 but are still living at 60. (Think about it)

You may not have been responsible for your heritage but you are responsible for your future.

Plan your work for today and every day. Then work your plan.

Luck is what happens when you prepare or practice. The more you prepare or practice, the luckier you get. Jim Imes

We make a living by what we get. We make a life by what we give.

The person who wins may have been counted out several times, but he didn't hear the referee.

When you cease to make a contribution you begin to die.

When a dog bites you the first time it isn't your fault. If the dog bites you again it is your fault.

We are smart and wise too late: and too old too soon. Jim Imes

To be a winner: all you have to do is give all you have.

Treasure the love you receive above all. It will survive long after your good health has vanished.

The mind, like a parachute, functions only when open.

Wisdom: the more sand that has escaped from the hourglass of life, the clearer we should see through it.

Those who bring good to others cannot keep it from themselves.

Act as though it were impossible to fail.

Love is life: if you miss love, you miss life.

Success is the distance between one's origins and one's final achievement.

Vision is the act of seeing the invisible.

Of all our human resources and instinct, the most precious is the desire to improve. Jim Imes

Opportunity rarely knocks on your door. Knock on opportunity's door if you wish to enter.

You cannot shake hands with a clenched fist. A person should give one another a firm hand shake. I like most of people appreciate a good handshake and believe a firm handshake means they are really sincere. In the case of a woman or children; don't hurt them with your handshake. I very much personally dislike it when a person shakes your hand with their fingertips like a wet noodle. This is just me. Jim Imes

About the only thing that comes without effort is old age.

You are only truly great if you are truly good.

Success doesn't come to you: you have to go to after it.

Be grateful for luck, but don't depend on it.

Of all the things you wear, your expression is the most important.

The surest way to go broke is to sit around waiting for a break.

A person dreams are an index to their greatness.

Money never starts the idea. The idea starts the money.

Choice, not chance, determines destiny.

Wisdom knows what to do next, skill knows how to do it, and virtue is doing it.

Believe as a child believes and magic will find you.

To an alcoholic, one drink is too many and 100 drinks aren't enough.

The same goes for cigarettes and drugs.

If it is good enough to read, then reread it and absorb it.

Wise men learn more from fools than fools learn from wise men.

The successful man will profit from his mistakes and try again in a different way.

To accomplish great things we must not only act, but also dream: not only plan, but also believe.

You can only make others better by being good yourself. You cannot change people unless they want to change. Jim Imes

The man who believes he can do something "can". And the one who believes he can't "won't".

There is no right way to do the wrong things.

You can measure a man by the size of his heart.

You can only make others better by being good yourself.

The smallest good deed is greater than the grandest intention.

The person that is good for making excuses is seldom good for anything else.

All your dreams can come true, if you have the courage to pursue them.

To win, you must treat a pressure situation as an opportunity to succeed, not as an opportunity to fail.

The first thing a person has to do to be any good at anything is to believe in himself. Then just let it go.

The best way to cheer yourself up is to cheer somebody else up.

Success is more attitude that than aptitude.

A friend walks in when everyone else walks out.

The next times you feel like grumbling just remember. Your garbage disposal eats better than 30% of the people that live in the world!

One thing you can give and still keep—is your word.

Success comes in cans. Failure comes in cants.

You are rich according to what you are, not according to what you have.

The best vitamin for making friends: B1

A smile is an inexpensive way to improve your looks.

Always keep reading and learning. It keeps you young; makes you smarter; slows down dementia; etc. Jim Imes

Behavior is the mirror in which everyone shows his or her image.

No man knows less than the man that knows it all.

Live your life as you wish your kids would.

It's nice to be important, but it's more important to be nice.

We lie loudest when we lie to ourselves.

He who forgives ends the quarrel.

Of all the things you wear, your expression is the most important.

Seek joy in what you give not is what you get.

Too many of us speak twice before we think.

Definition of a friend: a person who knows all about you and likes or loves you just the same.

When a man has done his best, has given his all, and in the process supplied the needs of his family and his society, that man has succeeded.

How are you going to be remembered when you die? Live a life that leaves a legacy that your friends and family will be proud of.

Have you noticed how people seem to read the Bible a whole lot more as they get older? Then it dawned on me . . . they were cramming for their finals! Jim Imes

What is important is not one's journey through life; but the lives one touches along that journey!

Life is too short to include people in your life that don't deserve it. Get rid of those negative people that seem like they are always trying to knock you off your pedestal of happiness. Jim Imes

THINGS YOU SHOULD KNOW BUT PROBABLY DON'T

1. Money isn't made out of paper; it's made out of cotton . . .
2. The Declaration of Independence was written on hemp (marijuana) paper.
3. The dot over the letter I am called a "tittle".
4. 315 entries in Webster's 1996 Dictionary were misspelled.
5. On average, 12 newborns will be given to the wrong parents, daily.
6. Chocolate affects a dog's heart and nervous system; a few ounces will kill a small sized dog.

7. Orcas (killer whales) kill sharks by torpedoing up into the shark's stomach from underneath, causing the shark to explode.

8. Most lipstick contains fish scales (ewe).

9. Upper and lower case letters are named 'upper' and 'lower' because in the time when all original print had to be set in individual letters, the upper case' letters were stored in the case on top of the case that stored the smaller, 'lower case' letters.

10. A tiny amount of liquor on a scorpion will make it instantly go mad and sting itself to death.

12. By raising your legs slowly and lying on your back, you can't sink in quicksand.

13. Celery has negative calories! It takes more calories to eat a piece of celery than the celery has in it to begin with. It's the same with apples!

14. Chewing gum while peeling onions will keep you from crying!

Chapter 3

WORK RELATED THOUGHTS

Business Sense

One of the biggest mistakes people make in management rolls is not gathering all the facts before responding to a situation. Even when the facts are gathered, some thought has to be applied before making hasty decisions or judgments! Jim Imes

Always nip a problem in the bud and do it in a very timely manner. Jim Imes

A bargain is anything a customer thinks the store is losing money on.

If the grass is greener somewhere else, then tend to the grass that's underneath your feet. (For those who always think the grass is greener somewhere else).

"There's never a wrong time to do the right thing, and never a right time to do the wrong thing."

Planning is a good thing. It wasn't raining when Noah was building the arc.

To handle yourself, use your head. To handle others, use your heart.

All people inclusive of customers, Managers, and fellow employees should follow this old adage to be successful. "Ladies & Gentlemen need to treat Ladies & Gentlemen like Ladies & Gentlemen!

If the going gets easy, you may be going downhill. (You may be coasting).

Every day do something nice at work and try not to get caught. Jim Imes

Know when to say something. Be a great listener! God gave you 2 ears and 1 mouth so that you can listen twice as much as you speak!

Are you part of the problem of part of the solution?

Failure is not the worst thing in the world. The very worst is not to try.

The aim of an argument or of discussion should not be victory, but progress.

To succeed: do the best you can, where you are, with what you have.

When a company consistently delivers superior value and wins customer loyalty, their market share and revenues go up, and the cost of acquiring and servicing customers goes down.

Service is the rent we pay for living. It is not something to do in your spare time: it is the very purpose of life.

First rule of holes: If you're in one, stop digging.

Don't complain about your problems. 80% of the people don't care, and the other 20% are glad you're having trouble.

Failure and mistakes are successes if we learn from it.

The Lord gave us two ends: one to sit on and the other to think with. Success depends on which one we use the most.

The price of greatness is responsibilities.

I always had a lot of patience when it came to business problems. The bigger the problem the more patience and control I had. It was the accumulation of a lot of smaller common sense problems that irritated me the most. Employees and customers were amazed at how much patience I showed towards them. Jim Imes

Some people never receive the honor they deserve and yet some people that don't deserve it receive it.

Always give credit to your employees because they are the ones that make you look good. Jim Imes

Don't be afraid to fail. Don't waste energy trying to cover up failure. Learn from your failures and go on to the next challenge. It's ok. If you're not failing, you're not growing.

One of the greatest victories you can gain over someone is to beat him or her at politeness.

Good is not good enough where better is expected.

Pray for what you want but work for the things you need.

If you are confused or unorganized, then the best you can expect from your employees or kids is confusion and un-organization. Jim Imes

The difference between greatness and mediocrity is often how an individual views a mistake.

Wise men learn more from fools, than fools from wise men.

Don't measure yourself by what you have accomplished, but by what you should have accomplished with your ability.

Nobody raises his own reputation by lowering others.

Life is a mirror, and we find only ourselves reflected in our associates.

God gives every bird its food, but He does not throw it into its nest.

Don't criticize anyone for 24 hours. And don't let your anger last more than 24 hours. I can be mad but after 24 hours I've thought about it and let it go. Jim Imes

Leadership means duty; honor your country, character, and it also means listening from time to time.

A visionary goal, thorough planning, dedicated execution, and total follow through can achieve personal excellence.

Obstacles are those frightful things you see when you take your eyes off of your goals.

Hold yourself responsible to a higher standard than anyone else expects of you.

People seldom improve when they have no other model but themselves to emulate.

Problems are only opportunities in work clothes.

Getting something done is an accomplishment: Getting something done right is an achievement.

Success is the maximum utilization of the ability you have.

You can't get much done by starting tomorrow.

Some people pay a compliment as if they expected a receipt.

I would rather see a mind opened by wonder than one closed by belief.

Don't follow the path. Go where there is no path and begin the trail. When you start a new trail equipped with courage, strength, and conviction, the only thing that can stop you is you.

If your actions create a legacy that inspires others to dream more, learn more, do more, and become more, then you are and excellent leader.

Pray for what you want, but work hard for the things you need.

Learn from the mistakes of others. You can't live long enough to make them all yourself.

The best executive is one who has sense enough to pick good people to do what he/she wants done, and self-restraint enough to keep from meddling, (micro managing), with them while they do it.

The tongue weighs practically nothing, but so few people can hold it.

Admit it when you make a mistake.

There are two kinds of people: those who do the work, and those who take the credit. Try to be in the first group. There is much less competition.

Always be on time. (5 minutes early is considered on time). Jim Imes

Co-operation is spelled with two letters-"we"

I am only one: but still I am one. I cannot do everything, but I can do something: I will not refuse to do something I can do!

The difference between ordinary and extra ordinary is that little extra effort.

One person has enthusiasm for 30 minutes: another for 30 days: but it is the man that has it for 30 years who makes a success of his life.

Opportunities are disguised by hard work; so most people don't recognize them.

We are continually faced by great opportunities brilliantly disguised as insolvable problems.

Hold yourself responsible a higher standard than anybody else expects of you. Never excuse yourself.

People seldom improve when they have no other model but themselves to copy after.

The harder you work, the luckier you get.

No one is useless in this world that lightens the burden of another.

If you aren't fired up with enthusiasm, you will be fired with enthusiasm.

Hire people smarter than you. This shows you're smarter than they are.

It's what you learn after you know everything that counts.

Many of life's failures are people who did not realize how close they were to success when they gave up.

Don't learn the tricks of the trade. Learn the trade.

Some people are like popcorn. You don't learn what they're really made of until you put heat under them.

Experience is a hard teacher. She gives the test first, the lesson afterwards.

Cultivate good manners, especially in business. Jim Imes

Our most important customer is you.

Anyone can sell products. We are not in the business of selling products.

We are in the business of selling service.

Asking a stupid question is better than correcting a stupid mistake. Hence the old saying, "there are no stupid questions".

The reward for work well done is the opportunity to do more.

Technology is great. I use Microsoft Outlook for more than email. I put daily, weekly, monthly, and yearly tasks and events in the calendar section of the program to remind me of things every day. For example: Did you exercise today? Did you clean the cat litter box and feed the fish? You can list doctor appointments; birthdays; and any other kind of reminder you want. And you can set them as reaccurances. It's called being organized.

Some Thought about Goals

If you don't know where you are going, how can you expect to get there? You need a map or goals.

Your present circumstances don't determine where you can go; they merely determine where you start.

The purpose of goals is to focus your attention on your future. Magic begins when you set them. Your power to accomplish becomes a reality when you have them.

Your mind reaches toward achievement when it has clear objectives.

Put your goals in writing. If you can't put it on a sheet of paper, you probably can't do it.

This one step: choosing a goal and sticking to it changes everything.

People with goals succeed because they know where they are going.

If what you are doing is not moving you towards your goals then it is moving you away from your goals.

There is no achievement without goals.

The most important thing about goals is having one.

A person without a plan is like a ship without a rudder.

Some Business Sense When Dealing With Employees

Rather than treating people equally, your goal should be to treat them *equitably.*

Frequently notice and reinforce the kind of behavior and performance you want from others.

In the long run, you'll be much better off using your best resources (employees) in areas of strength rather than problem zones.

Employees, customers, colleagues, and business partners are our only important assets!

With few exceptions, different isn't wrong . . . it's just different.

You don't manage people, you *lead* them. You manage the department.

The difference between a Manager and a Leader is: In WWII the manager was the Admiral on the ship managing where the guns would be fired. The leader was the Captain or Sargent that was leading his troops under fire to the beach. Jim Imes

The only time people know what you're thinking is when you tell them.

It's not enough to just know your values, you need to *behave* them . . . you need to walk the talk.

One surefire way to succeed in business and life is to treat people the way they want to be treated.

When dealing with performance problems, focus on problem solving and correction rather than punishment.

Look for and create opportunities to learn, grow, and continually improve.

Encourage people to have fun, enjoy their work, and think.

Lasting change doesn't come from doing a little a lot better. It comes from doing a lot a little better.

The best developmental feedback is frequent, informal, and comes from multiple sources. And sometimes this is the people that work in the pit; your employees. Jim Imes

Everyone is responsible for his or her own behavior.

Empathy means wallowing awhile in someone else's shoes. It's about being considerate and understanding.

Rules should be followed or changed, but not <u>ignored</u>.

If people don't meet expectations, find out why. Then choose an appropriate response. Don't assume training is the answer.

Never forget your ideas, write them down.

Phases to Forget That Stifle Creativity and Initiative Never Say or Think These Words

♦ It doesn't matter what I do . . . I'm only one person.
♦ I'll change just as soon as everyone else does.

- That's their opinion . . . what do they know?
- Because I said so, that's why.
- Do as I say, not as I do.
- It's not my job.
- We've tried that before.
- That'll never work.
- They'll never let us do that.
- I already know how it will turn out.
- That's not how I would do it.
- We've always done it that way.
- Nobody else does it that way.
- We've got more than enough good ideas.
- Whose idea was this, anyway?
- "They didn't get back to me." or, "they are getting back to me." both are equally disastrous. Expecting someone to get back to you stops the action. Take the initiative.
- "I thought someone else was taking care of that." excuses indicate a roadblock to action. Always ask questions to keep things moving.
- "No one ever told me." or, "it's not my job." or "I don't feel like it right now." let a supervisor hear you talk this way very often and you will have made a very clear statement about the way you work. You operate in a tunnel, oblivious to everything that is going on around you.
- "I didn't think to ask about that." an inability to see down the road may indicate that you lack the ability to understand and grasp relationships.

in business today is clear. The
re for success is performance.
er the roadblocks, it's your job to
ve them. If not, you'll be perceived as
e of the roadblocks.

Code of Ethics for Employees

♦ Truth: we will make accurate claims to our customers, use only competent testimonials, and strive to be open about all aspects of the products or services we offer.

♦ Honesty: We will uphold the highest degree of honesty towards our customers and each other. We shall uphold the principles of professionalism and fair play.

♦ Integrity: We will abide by all the laws and strive to serve our customers with honest values. We will avoid using all devises and schemes, which prey on human ignorance or gullibility.

♦ Cooperativeness: We will support each other in a team effort. We will cooperate with our customers, businesses, and each other.

♦ Self-accountability: We will honor all commitments including any guarantees we offer. We will seek to resolve, in a fair and expeditious manner any disputes, which may rise.

♦ Be genuinely respectful and considerate of all guests and fellow employees.

- Be consistently on time to work ar meetings. If you don't then you are a _ro_ of other people's valuable time.
- Be clean, well groomed, and professiona appearance.
- Be responsible and accountable for your ow actions.
- Be a dedicated team player.
- Be consistently friendly.
- Be sincerely concerned about the welfare of the customers and each other.
- Be obsessively dedicated to giving excellent service.
- Be genuinely patient, understanding, and tolerant.
- Totally support the efforts of each other.
- Continually contribute to a clean, safe, secure environment.
- Take ownership of an issue until it is resolved.
- Understand that your actions contribute to the strength and value of the company.
- Be an attentive listener and accurately communicate to and between all levels.
- Be technically proficient in your job.
- Use the 10 foot greeting/acknowledgement rule. Anyone that comes within 10 feet of you gets acknowledged and or greeted with a smile.
- Always be in control of your emotions when dealing with customers and each other at work.
- Realize that your opinions and actions are a reflection of the company.

♦ Maintain a positive attitude in the workplace.
♦ Be familiar with your basic company's information including history, style, core ethics, and their mission statement.

As an Employee You Have Several Responsibilities to Your Employer

♦ To perform a good day's work
♦ To be loyal
♦ To act as part of the team
♦ To value the relationship
♦ To earn the employer's trust
♦ To grow with a passion for the product/service

Philosophy of a Leader

A manager once said to a trainer, "My biggest problem with training is, what if you invest a lot in the employee to train them to your business practices, and they leave you for another company?" The trainer's reply was, *"What if you don't train them, and they stay?"*

Our Customer

Our customer is the most important person around here . . . in person, by phone or by letter.

Our customer can get along without us . . . but we cannot get along without him.

Our customer is not interfering with our work . . . he is the reason for it. Service to him is not a favor from us; his giving us a chance to serve is a favor from him.

Our customer is not a number on a list . . . he is a person, entitled to likes and dislikes and human feelings, even as you and I.

Our customer is not someone to try to out-smart or out-argue. Winning the argument means losing the customer.

Our customer is someone we ask to bring us his needs. It is our responsibility to take care of them to our mutual gain.

Our customer is not always right . . . but the customer is always the customer. Right or wrong, they are the lifeblood of your business and they must be treated as the lifeblood of your business.

Handling the Hostile Customer

You can't please all the customers all the time. But how you handle hostile customers speaks volumes about your business.

Treat problem customers right, you'll earn their repeat business . . . not to mention the referrals they may send your way. Brush them off, and you'll lose both.

The experts say the best way to deal with problem customers is to treat complaints as compliments. Promptly thank the customer for coming forward, and explain how their feedback helps you make changes to improve your service.

Then find a quiet place and listen carefully to the complaint without interrupting. Once the customer is finished, confirm that you understand the problem and offer to make amends.

During this exchange, it's important that you remain calm, you'll get nowhere by arguing, making excuses or shifting the blame. You must take a hostile customer's complaint head-on to maintain your credibility.

Also remember angry customer's sometimes just want to vent their frustrations. But if after blowing off some steam they're still piqued, be prepared to offer them a refund, discount, or apology letter on the spot.

Types of Customers

The satisfied customers are easy to deal with.

The dissatisfied customer is a challenge to us.

The potential customer is influenced by our attitude.

A satisfied customer tells 3 others about our good service.

A dissatisfied customer tells 11 others about our bad service.

Ten Commandments of good customer service

1. A customer is the most important person in any business
2. A customer is not dependent of us. We are dependent on the customer
3. A customer is not an interruption of our work, but rather the purpose of it.
4. A customer does a favor by calling; we are not doing them a favor by serving him or her.
5. A customer is part of our business, not an outsider.
6. A customer is a human being with feelings and emotions like us.
7. A customer is not someone to argue or match wits with.
8. A customer is a person who brings us needs; it is our job to fill those needs.
9. A customer is deserving of the most courteous and attentive treatment we can give.
10. A customer is the lifeblood of every business.

Why do customers leave?

1% = die

3% = move or relocate to other areas

8% = form other loyalties

16% = go to competitors

14% = dissatisfied with the product

58% = leave because of the attitude of the employees of the company!

Tonality and Body Language

Have you ever met an employee that say have a good day but their voice and body language doesn't reflect any sincerity? You can tell if they are saying it because they were told to by their employers or if they really mean it. I love it when an employee is sincere, it makes you feel good that you did business with that establishment.

Customer Defection Statistics

For the average company, customers defect at the rate of 10% to 30% per year. Over time, this disloyalty stunts performance by 25% to 50%.

In contrast, an increase of just 5% in customer loyalty can result in 25% to 85% more profit.

It costs 5 times as much to acquire a new customer as it costs to service an existing customer.

What Customers Want!
Some things you need to know:

You have to be passionate about your business.

The customer may not always be right, but let him or her be wrong with dignity.

The customer is not always right, but the customer is and will always be the customer.

There are no stupid questions but there are a lot of stupid excuses or answers. Jim Imes

Always point with multiple fingers or your whole hand, it is much less threatening. Never point with one finger!

Facts are negotiable; perceptions are not. What is the customer's perception of you, our business, and etc. fact: a customer can get product anywhere. What makes them come here?

We have thousands of unpaid consultants every year. Why wouldn't we listen to them? Why would we ever say or do anything to lose their loyalty?

Treat every person as a V.I.P. <u>Very Individual Person</u>.

What Makes a Customer Come to a Place of Business?

Do you have the product?

Aesthetics: is the place clean? (You can judge a business by its restrooms). Is it orderly, nice to visit, and easy to park, etc.?

It makes no difference if you are hired as a vice president or a hot dog vendor the first thing you should learn to do is to pick up trash. Then you learn your regular duties. If a vice president or manager steps over a piece of trash the first one to notice is fellow employees. What message does that send out? They should also wipe off the sink and surrounding area after they wash their hands or splashed water and soap to keep it looking nice and profession. Clean up after yourself, it's the right thing to do! The customers will notice. Also a newly hired employee should work 3 days in each department prior to starting to work in the department that they were hired. Jim Imes

The actual buy and the price are third on the list. People will pay for value if the perception is good.

Do not promise what you cannot deliver. It's the fastest way to lose a loyal customer.

Customers are "guests". What is the first thing you do when you find out someone is coming over to your home? (You clean it). Why would you do less at the place you spend more awake hours than at home?

Are You a Coaster?

Companies go out of business by just maintaining or coasting.

Do you know how to tell if a person is going to win a bicycle race? Look for the one that when he reaches the top of the hill he keeps pedaling even when he is going downhill. The ones who get to the top of the hill and pats themselves on the back for the great effort they just made going up the hill and then coasts down the hill is not the one who is going to win. You have to be proactive.

Some Telephone Basic's

What are the basic rules for answering the telephone?

Pick us the telephone within 3 rings, greet the caller, give your name, and ask if you may be of assistance.

What are the basic rules for putting a customer on hold? Ask the customer if it's ok to place them on hold, wait for an answer, tell the customer why they are being placed on hold, give them a timeframe, and thank them when you return.

Wise Words

The greatest Joy	Giving
The greatest loss	Loss of self-respect
The most satisfying work	Helping others
The ugliest personality trait	Selfishness
The most endangered species	Dedicated leaders
Our greatest natural resource	Our youth
The greatest "shot in the arm"	Encouragement
The greatest problem to overcome	Fear
The most effective sleeping pill	Peace of mind
The most crippling failure disease	Excuses
The most powerful force in life	Love
The most dangerous pariah	A gossiper
The world's most incredible computer	The brain
The worst thing to be without	Hope

The deadliest weapon	The tongue
The two most power-filled words	"I Can"
The greatest asset!	Faith
The most worthless emotion	Self-pity
The most beautiful attire	A SMILE!
The most prized possession	Integrity
The most powerful channel of communication	Prayer
The most contagious spirit	Enthusiasm
The most destructive habit	Worry

Chapter 4

WHAT I HAVE LEARNED, BUT NOT ALL THAT I HAVE LEARNED

I will start out with some personal stories that gave me the Street Smarts and Wisdom I acquired with age.

Some of my early life lessons didn't mature in my mind until later in life. This is important because I never forgot the lesson, and when it did mature I tried to pass these lessons in life onto my children so they wouldn't have to actually experience them themselves.

I learned later in life that not everything I, or for that matter other people think or have an opinion on will not always be the same. It all depends on how they were raised and influenced, and on the morals and values they were taught. Just look at how much people disagree on religion; politics; war; and every other conceivable subject they are passionate about. It seems everyone has an opinion on something. Even subjects they know nothing about. And there is always going to be disagreements on certain subjects depending on your beliefs; morals; and values. This is true even when you have the proof and the facts to support otherwise, which proves that some people are just thick headed and stubborn. It's seems to be human nature for some people to do so. Some people are so passionate with their own beliefs and opinions that again I will say that they can be blind and deaf to the facts.

When a child is born, he or she is nothing short of a miracle. They can be anything you program them to be. A baby is born with an empty mind, per say. It is very similar to a formatted hard drive in a computer. When he or she is born the only way they know how to communicate is to cry or fuss. They use this method to tell you they are hungry; they are uncomfortable with their messy diaper; they don't feel good; etc. They are amazing little sponges that will absorb anything you teach them. Like a computer in which you can type and program, everything you as parents teach them will reflex in the type of person they will grow up to be. And of course they are also programed by other family members; teachers; and all the people they come in contact with in their early lives. They say that a child learns all of their values, morals, and traits by the time they are 8 years old. <u>Good or bad</u>.

Having a baby is the most important responsibility you will ever have, bar none. It is the parent or parents responsibility to insure that their child have all the tools necessary to survive in today's world. I believe the number one thing you can teach a child to survive is to be independent instead of the alternative of being dependent or co-dependent. That is unless your goal is for your children to live with you, depend, and support them for the rest of your life. It will be your job, especially in the formative years to them an education; teach them the difference between right and wrong, good and bad; teach them respect; (accept nothing less than respect from your children. Reverend Billy Graham once said, "If you don't discipline a child then that child will not respect anyone when they grow up."); teach them great morals and values; teach them etiquette and manners; teach them that lying will not be tolerated and that honesty will be self-rewarding; teach them to be positive; teach them to share; teach them not to hate; teach them to forgive, (forgiveness is what Christianity is built on); teach them to follow their dreams, (not your dreams); teach them patriotism and how to be a good citizen; teach them about God and let them decide when they are 18 years or older to decide about religion. Teach them to cook; balance a checkbook; clean up after themselves; teach them to be organized; teach them to sing; teach them to dance, to love themselves, etc.

In other words teach them everything they will need to survive in this world and you will have done your job as a great parent. One of my great role models was my grandfather Verle Imes. He was a person of integrity and a gentleman of the 1st degree. I have tried very hard to model myself after him.

Side Notes about programming a child.

Did you ever wonder why there are so many people in the world that hate Americans and other countries of the world that are free? These people who hate freedom and democracy and what it represents in America have programed their children from the time of their birth to hate us and the freedoms we represent. The children believe with all their hearts that killing and hating the people that their parents and grandparents have hated for generations is a good thing, a religious thing. They have been <u>brain washed/programed</u> this since birth. That is why they have no problem killing innocent people as a suicide bomber, etc. We as Americans could do that to our children too, but fortunately for us we live in in a free country, and our fore fathers had the fore site to base our government on common sense and Christian values, and the greatest Constitution and Bill of Rights, bar none, than any other country in the world! We are not raised to hate any nation or religion. Of that I'm sure.

Baby Boomers and Pre Baby Boomers

I believe that Baby Boomers and Pre Baby Boomers are and were and still are the smartest; toughest; most street wise people that ever lived. They went through two World Wars; Korean War; Mexican/American War; Vietnam War; and the Great Depression. I believe that a lot of the X and Y generations, also known as the Me Generation, (me, me, me, me, me), or Microwave Generation, (they want it right now, even if they can't afford it), have taken for granted the freedoms and rights that were given to them by the blood of their ancestors. They seem to feel entitled. I'm not saying that they are all this way, not by a long shot, but it is the tendency of a parent to give to their children more than they received growing up. We of the Baby Boomer Generation are at fault that some of our children have turned out this way. It seems like we are drifting farther and farther away from God; patriotism; our Constitution and Bill of Rights; common sense; and have taken for granted that we were once, (it's questionable now days), the greatest Nation on Earth.

Growing up in the Fifties and Early Sixties

Now let's talk about growing up in the fifties and sixties, and how discipline played a role in shaping us into the people we are today. Discipline in the fifties and sixties included a spanking from our parents and was acceptable then but now is considered by some to be child abuse. It was an acceptable practice in those days to get a spanking as it was with many earlier generations dating back for hundreds and thousands of years. We were not beaten within an inch of our lives. We were disciplined. We were spanked on the fat of our butt with a hand, switch, paddle, or a belt. Not on the arms, legs, or face. Sure it stung, but more than that it seemed to hurt our pride. We cried, but in exchange we learned to respect our parents and that our actions had consequences.

Today some people believe in a time out versus a good spanking, and think it's wrong to spank a child, and then they wonder why their child grows up without respect for anyone. They scream at their parents. They are uncontrollable in school; the super market; they throw tantrums; they don't mind; they are spoiled brats; etc.

In the fifties and sixties your friend's parents were allowed to spank you and they did if you were bad. And you knew you were going to get disciplined again when you got home. I went to Catholic school from the 1st through the 6th grades and yes they took a flat ruler a rapped your knuckles when you were disrupting the class. They put you in the corner on a stool facing the corner; clean the chalk boards after class; or write a 100 times the lesson they were trying to impart to you. And it was perfectly alright with your parents. God forbid if they did that nowadays.

Restriction in our generation meant you were confined to your room. No friends. No phone. No TV. No radio. You could play with your little plastic army men or dolls if you were a girl, read or draw, but you definitely knew you were being punished. Unlike today's generation where the kids have cell phones; TV's in their room; Xbox or Play Stations; computers; IPods; Stereos; etc., are not taken away during the restriction. What kind of punishment is that? What kind of message does that send to a child?

Answer: Restriction isn't so bad. I don't even feel like I'm being punished. And when our parents said you were on restriction for a week, you weren't let off early for good behavior no matter how much you begged. It was punishment. It wasn't supposed to be fun.

Also I have to say that growing up in the fifties and sixties we had great television programs. To me it seems all of the programs had great scripts and plots. They were family programs. They would all be considered PG. Some of my favorites were: Rin Tin Tin; Lassie; Flipper; The Red Skelton Show; Bonanza; Gunsmoke; Father Knows Best; Mr. Ed; Sea Hunt; The Honeymooners; The Lone Ranger; and so many more. And may I add that in the fifties we only had 4 channels and most of us could only afford a Black and White TV. Each of these shows were either funny or their theme was to teach a lesson. We were educated in morals; values, manners; and right or wrong.

The children of the X and Y generations wouldn't watch these shows. Not enough violence; action; special effects; killing; etc. I want to state that I love most of today's television and movies. I love technology and the fact that we now have more choices of what we can watch. We have hundreds of channels and almost always I can find something interesting to watch. I love most of the educational programs and cartoons that children watch now. I love the History Channel; Syfy; TNT; Bio; Modern Marvels; Military Channel; Disney; CMT; FNC; and more. I could do without all the channels that sell nothing but products.

And yes in the fifties and sixties they threatened to keep kids back a grade if they failed. Some students weren't as smart as others, so they failed a grade and were held back to repeat the same grade. Tests were not adjusted or graded on a curve for any reason.

No one ever asked where the car keys were because they were always in the car, in the ignition, the visor, or the glove compartment, and the doors were never locked?

When being sent to the principal's office was nothing compared to the fate that awaited the student at home? Basically we were in fear for our lives, but it wasn't because of drive-by shootings, drugs, gangs, etc. Our parents and grandparents were a much bigger threat! But we survived because their love was greater than the threat.

And yes we all drank from the same hose. We asked to go out and play and Moms said to be home at dinner or when the street lights come on.

We would pick up a penny from the muddy curb.

Our baby cribs were covered with bright colored lead-based paint. And we survived.

We had no childproof lids on medicine bottles, doors, or cabinets. And when we rode our bikes, we had no helmets. (Not to mention the risks we took hitchhiking.)

As children, we would ride in cars with no seat belts or airbags. Riding in the back of a pickup truck on a warm day was always a special treat.

We ate cupcakes, bread and butter, and drank soda pop with sugar in it, but we were never overweight because we were always outside playing.

We shared one soft drink with four friends, from one bottle, and no one actually died from this.

We played with toy guns, some looked very real. Sometimes we made them ourselves; we used wood and rubber bands. But we didn't grow up killing other people.

We would spend hours building our go-carts out of scraps and then rode down the hill, only to find out we forgot the brakes. After running into the bushes a few times, we learned to solve the problem.

We had friends! We went outside and found them.

We played dodge ball, and sometimes, the ball would really hurt.

We fell out of trees, got cut, and broke bones and teeth, and there were no lawsuits from these accidents. They were accidents. No one was to blame but us. <u>Remember accidents</u>?

We had fights and punched each other and got black and blue and learned to get over it.

We made up games with sticks and tennis balls and ate worms and swallowed watermelon seeds, and although we were told it would happen, we did not put out very many eyes, nor did the worms live inside us forever and not one watermelon seed sprouted.

We rode bikes or walked to a friend's home and knocked on the door, or rang the bell or just walked in and talked to them.

Little League had tryouts and not everyone made the team. Those who didn't had to learn to deal with disappointment.

Our actions were our own. Consequences were expected. The idea of a parent bailing us out if we broke the law was unheard of. They actually sided with the law.

The Baby Boomer generation has produced some of the best risk-takers, problem solvers, and inventors, ever. The past 50 years have been an explosion of innovation and new ideas.

We had freedom, failure, success, and responsibility, and we learned how to deal with it all.

Side story about siding with the law

My youngest son Ryan got into trouble with the law. He broke the law and voluntarily turned himself in to the Police. He was not eligible for bail and I would not have bailed him out regardless, because I believe a person should pay for his crimes and learn all lessons related to breaking the law. He had to spend 90 days in jail. In that time my current Wife Carla and I would visit him as did his Mom. He picked up a Bible and read it while he was in jail. He told us how much he hated jail and when he finally got out he was a different person. It was like a light went on in his mind. He changed his ways and no longer hung out with the kids that got him in trouble. So you see now why parents during the forties; fifties; and sixties *sided with the law.*

I loved the fifties and sixties.

Lesson: When I was 6 years old in 1957 and living in South Pasadena, California, I was playing in our back yard. Our family lived in the front house and my grandparents lived in the house behind us on the same lot. Being a 6 year old bored child and wanting for something to do I found a 4 foot half inch round metal cable wire lying on the ground and began throwing it in the air to see how high I could throw it.

Well back in those days not all electric cables were run underground. We had one running to our front house from the street power Pole and another from our house to my grandparents' house behind us. The metal cable I was throwing up into the air landed on the electrical cable that was running between the two houses. The electric cable broke and as chance would have it, it landed on an old cloth couch sitting in our back yard.

Sparks were flying from the end of the downed cable and lit the couch on fire. The power line was jumping all over the place to the length of the electrical line and was a danger to anyone close to it.

My mother saw what happened and called the Fire Department. The Fire Department and the Police came and I believe later the electric company. They controlled it and repaired it, but I was in big trouble. Because of my carelessness the electricity to both homes were cut off for a time and my parents had to pay for the repair. I got a good lecture coupled with a whipping from my dad; along with a week's worth of restriction.

My family of 5 was not rich. In fact we spent most of our life as a lower middle class family. We never lacked the necessities to live, but we also didn't have any extra money for emergencies.

I never forgot this event in my life and the lesson I learned was my carelessness could have burned down one of the houses and someone could have gotten critically hurt along with the expense my parents had to put out. Again I should also say that a lot of my early lessons in life didn't fully mature in my mind until I got older. But I never forgot them.

Lessons I learned playing team sports.

When I was 8 years old I joined Little League. I had already loved the game as I played at the Recreation Center and at school with my friends. As an 8 year old in an 8 to 10 year old league I only got to play 1 inning because the 9 and 10 year olds were better and Little League required that each child had to play a minimum of one inning. I was pretty good fielding the ball but lacked on hitting. Those 10 year old pitchers threw pretty hard. I was satisfied and just happy to practice and play when I could. But I learned you had to start somewhere and my time would come.

When I was 10 years old I was one of the better players on the team. I could play every position except catcher. I was rather a small kid until I hit High School. In this one game I hit a ball over the right fielder's head and went into 3rd base along with the throw. The ball got by the 3rd baseman and I ran home. It was a bang-bang play and I slid hard into the catcher. The umpire called me out, but I saw that the catcher didn't catch the ball; in fact it was underneath my back. I got up and gave the ball to the umpire and he didn't change his call. I went back to the dugout and started to cry. The coach came over to console me but he never stood up for me with the umpire. I never understood why but the lesson I learned is _life is not always fair_.

I play baseball up until I was 15. I played in the Babe Ruth league from ages 13 to 15. I like a lot of kids dreamed of being a baseball player. I was an excellent player, one of the best in the league. But my dream got squashed when I was 16. I had matured enough by the time I was 16, (I had to grow up fast and be responsible), and to realize how much my parents had to struggle just to get by with 3 sons. My parents couldn't afford anything extra in the way of uniforms; cleats; glove; bat; or entry fees for the team, so I didn't even try out. It ended up this way with all sports for me in high school and I never got to play high school sports. They couldn't even afford year books for me. I learned to deal with disappointments.

A Chicken Soup story about a Little League team I coached.

I coached Little League and Babe Ruth for 5 years but the 5th year almost didn't happen. The first year I coach Little League was as an assistant coach to Ken Sherman who had a son that was 9 years old, Bradley Sherman. I was 21 and young enough that the kids could relate to me. I got asked to coach Babe Ruth ages 13 to 15 the next year and I basically followed the 13 year olds until they turned 15 and then I wanted to retire from coaching. I never had worse than a 2nd place team and again I think because of my youth and because I had such a great background in the sport of baseball we succeeded.

I was at work one day at Barber Ford and the Parts Manager, Kenny Heath asked me if I would coach his sons Little League team. His son was 10 years old which would mean that I would have to go back to coaching 8 to 10 year old kids. A lot of work compared to coaching the older boys. Kenny pleaded with me and said that if I didn't coach his son's team that 13 kids would not get to play that year. I finally said yes when he said that I could take off of work early to coach the team. I asked him when the try outs were and he laughed. (A try out for those of you that don't know is when you can look at the players throwing balls; fielding grounders; catching fly balls; and batting, etc.)

The reason he laughed is that he told me that try outs were already done and these were the kids that no other team wanted, Ha! I held my first practice and met the team. Much to my surprise they consisted of more little girls than boys. I wasn't very optimistic about winning very many games, but much to my surprise there were 2 standouts that had signed up late, a boy and a girl that turned out to be key players. The little girl could pitch and catch and the little boy could pitch and catch. They were both 10 year olds with great arms. At this level of Little League pitching was 90% of the game. I also had some 8 year boys and girls that knew nothing about baseball. I had to teach them how to throw; how to catch; the rules; and how to hit.

There was one little boy whose mother came up to me and told me her son never had a father figure and was afraid of the ball, etc. I worked especially hard with him and made him our right fielder as this position usually got the least amount of action. We went through the season and on the last game of the season we were tied with the other team for first place. The other team was very good. The coach and I knew that they were better than ours but with some outstanding pitching and some luck we could win.

It was a close game and we were up one run going into the bottom of the last inning. There were 2 outs and kids on second and third base. I had put the child I talked about earlier into right field, (I'm sorry I don't remember his name), and the batter hit a long fly ball to right field that would have of won the game but wait: my player didn't have to move an inch. You couldn't hear a thing from the crowd of parents watching because they knew this child and his abilities. He closed his eyes and opened his glove and the ball went into his glove and he caught it for the 3rd out. The fans cheered. It was really a miracle to me. It happened exactly that way.

The league couldn't afford trophies so the Parts Manager and I bought them inexpensive trophies and gave them each a trophy at Pizza celebration party. I learned that no matter what kind of hand your dealt. You could make it a great hand by believing and a little help from above.

One of the biggest lessons I ever learned was when I was about 10 years old. I hung around with a girl named Judy and she and I were walking home from the Recreation Center one day when a boy and his sister started throwing small rocks at us. We returned fire with small rocks and were definitely getting the better of them. The sister saw this and got her brother a huge rock to throw. Way too large for the distance we were apart. He tried throwing the rock and his sister was standing in front of him and little to the right and he hit her right in the eye.

His sister ran into the house and told her parents that we had thrown the rock, which was a big lie. We told their parents and our parents that it was a lie. Of course their parents didn't believe us. I had gotten into trouble so much that the Police took me to the jail and showed me empty jail cells. They asked me if I wanted to end up here and of course I was scared to death and said no. Needless to say I had learned my lesson about getting in trouble and never ever, even in my teen age years got into trouble with the Police again. I became a model citizen.

Physical Fitness

I graduated Buena High School in 1969. President John F. Kennedy had enacted a program that all high school students would take physical tests for a month. We did two physical tests a day in gym class. There were tests like running the 50 and 100 yard dash; running the 440 and a mile. Climbing the peg board and climbing a 25 foot rope. How many sit ups and push ups you could do in 60 seconds. Swim the 100 meters in the fastest time. How many dips you could do on the parallel bars? How many pull ups and chin ups you could do; and how far you could throw a softball, etc.

What the school did was paint numbers outside the gym from 1 to 200 and based on the scores you got on the tests, you stood on your number for the rest of the semester. I ranked 4th in a class of Seniors, Juniors, and Sophomores. In the next semester I ranked 2nd.

Why am I telling you this? After 1967 they stopped doing this program: Why? I can only speculate. I think it was because too many lazy students didn't want to do it anymore, or their parents thought it was somehow unfair. But I loved it and it gave me a gauge as to how fit I was. I loved gym class. I loved being fit. It was a great program and in my opinion be reinstated. I learned that American children and teen agers are getting soft. They are out of shape. The parents created this problem and the parents should fix it at home and in the schools. Don't let your kids sit around and get fat. About 27 percent of children ages 6 to 18 are obese. And the percent of children that are overweight is much higher. When I went to school you hardly ever saw anyone that was heavy.

Lesson about Fire, Responsibility, and Truth

When I was 9 years old my brother and I did something very dumb. We had a crawl way underneath our house that was about 4 feet tall. My younger brother and I went down there one day and decided to make a campfire. Well the smoke went into the house and my Mom panicked and called the Fire Department.

My brother got cold feet and went and told my Mom that I had lit the fire under the house. I put out the fire and ran as far as I could away from home. A motorcycle Policeman found me and asked me if I was Jimmy Imes. I lied and gave him some fake name but I didn't know that my Mom had showed a picture of me to the Policeman. The only fun I got out this adventure was riding back to the house on his motorcycle. I got a pretty bad spanking and a month's worth of restriction. After that I learned how dangerous my actions were and that lying didn't work. I got in trouble for that too.

Catholic School

I would like you all to know what it was like for me growing up Catholic. I went to Catholic school through the 6th grade. I became a perfectionist because of the way that the nuns went taught school. I was also influenced by my mother and my Uncle Bruce in perfectionism.

My Mom was a great home maker and was born in Holland. Before I was born my Mom used to iron everything of my dad's, including his underwear. She stopped doing that when I was born because raising children is a full time job.

I also learned to be a perfectionist from my Uncle Bruce. He is extremely organized and takes great care of everything he ever owned. People would love to own one of the many vehicles he owned throughout his lifetime. It might be 10 years old but it looked and ran like new. His house is always spotless. He hangs his clothes in his closets 2 fingers apart. His cabinets for all his food and dishes are extremely organized. You could live in his garage it's so clean.

But back to the Sisters and Catholic school. When we were taught something they demanded perfection, especially when it came to hand writing. We used that paper with the solid lines on the top and bottom and the dash lines in the middle. You had to make your letters, if you were printing, to perfectly fit on the lines. The Capital letters had to touch the top and bottom lines, and the small letters had to touch the dashed line and the bottom line. You had to make your letters exactly the way they were displayed above the chalk board. I used to always have a problem with the small K's, Ha! And when we learned to write in cursive, we used to do these exercises of continuous O's and if they were not perfect you had to do them over and over again until they were.

I came out of Catholic school with great hand writing. I was and have been proud of it for most of my life now. I very much dislike when people use some sort of custom signature that nobody can read. I used to get complimented all the time on my hand writing. It is a little shaky now that I'm 62, but very legible. The Sisters were this way in everything they taught. As a parent you always had the confidence that they were teaching your children not only about English, Math, History, etc., but they were also teaching them the correct morals and values that they would use for the rest of their lives. I have since learned not to be a perfectionist in my personal life because a lot of people were uncomfortable with it. My perfectionism; being anal; maybe manic; would drive both of my ex-wives crazy. I had to change to seeking excellence. I realized later on in life that perfection wasn't possible. <u>Even Jesus wasn't perfect!</u>

Success in Business

I believe I said it earlier that I was a little smaller than other kids my age. It wasn't until I was 16 that I had a growth spurt to 5'10" tall. I didn't grow any more after that. But I did discovered when it comes to choosing players that I was always one of the ones that were picked last whenever we chose teams. I also learned that nobody ever wanted to be the captain so I started volunteering to be captain. This helped me later in life to become a great leader and handle responsibility.

I knew the abilities of all the kids and more times than not I picked the winning team. I went on to coaching Little League, Babe Ruth baseball, softball, and when I was 32 years old I became a Lincoln Mercury Parts Manager. I was one of the most successful Ford/Lincoln Mercury Parts Manager in the United States for 30 years.

I took what I learned from being a team captain and converted it into business lessons. I taught my employees how to work as a team. I trained them personally and then just let them do their job. I didn't micro-manage but I did *inspect what I expected* from them. I put their jobs in the simplest form because one of the keys to success in business is simplicity. And because I learned the business of Parts from the bottom to the top, I was able to teach each of my employees everything they needed to learn to be successful.

Sports: Sports in general is anything that requires you get off your duff and do something. It could be climbing; running; walking; football; baseball; soccer; tennis; golf; darts; racket ball; anything. But this is the advice I would give everyone. You've all heard the saying, "Practice makes perfect". Well that is so wrong. Practice makes permanent. That is why everyone should learn from a qualified person or coach about the proper techniques for playing certain sports. If you practice the wrong way then you are just practicing bad habits which become permanent. This is so important in complicated games like golf. If you don't learn from a professional then you can practice for years and never get any better. Remember: *Practice make permanent*.

I've learned that America is not a place for your fresh garbage I have seen far too many people trashing up America. Tagging buildings and bridges; throwing trash out of their vehicles; dumping trash on empty lots; dumping trash in the lakes and ocean; etc. It's so sad to think that some Americans think so little of this great country that they do that.

My former boss Tom Coward told us story about a friend of his. They were both multi millionaire's but Mr. Coward told all the managers at a meeting that his friend owned a huge office complex and that every day he would park as far away as he could and pick up the trash on his way to his office. The point is he was a millionaire and didn't have to do this, but he cared enough that he wanted to do it. Did I also mention he was in his mid-seventies?

I now park far away at the grocery store for both the exercise and cart return area is usually toward the end of the parking lot. I will pick up plastics and aluminum. I also walk my dog 1.2 miles almost every day and I pick up trash, plastic, and aluminum.

I walk 1.2 miles every morning with my dog and I pick recyclable trash that people throw on the ground and bring it home and put it in my recycle can.

I am a recycling nut. It takes anywhere from 100 years to thousands of years, depending on what kind of plastic you are talking about to decompose. Glass never decomposes. If you truly care for your children, grandchildren, and great grandchildren then I think you should recycle.

Pets: I've learned that pets can extend a person's life. I've learned that some people need pets to survive emotionally. I've learned that pets will love you no matter what. I've learned that pets are just like children and have to be taken care of like children. Fact: 90% of the pets in Europe are trained and trained well. 75% of the pets in America are not trained at all. I've learned that you should never own a pet unless you can physically and financially take care of that pet from the minute you own it until the minute it passes away. You have to be able to pay for food, healthcare, and clean up after them <u>daily</u> just like you would if they were your own children. If you get a pet because your children requested you to do so then make sure that they understand that they have to take care of that pet too if they are old enough. And if they are not old enough then teach them when they are.

Music: My Mom and dad bought a used standup piano when I was 8 years old. It was in rough shape. I think they paid $15 for it. My dad sanded it all down and refinished it dark brown. They had it tuned.

My parents enrolled me in piano lessons at Catholic School and I learned to play the piano well enough to be in the school recital. I played two songs and got through them without a mistake.

Learning to play the piano was one of the best things that my parents could have ever done for me. It introduced me to music and at 15 years old I picked up the guitar and have been playing guitar for 46 years now.

I think that all parents should encourage their children to learn some sort of instrument. They will thank you for the rest of their lives. I was also in the Church Choir. The Sister that ran the choir told me that I had a very good voice. I encourage parents to teach their children to sing as it will bring joy to both them and you. By the way, all people can learn to sing. Just like sports it requires vocal exercises and practice.

Event Tracker and Journal

I have learned that everyone should keep a journal of their life. I'm not talking about a young teen's diary, but an <u>event tracker</u>. There are so many things you learn in your lifetime. There are so many events that happen in your lifetime. There are so many people that you meet and that influenced you and you have forgotten timelines and names. I just want to encourage everyone that it's never too late to start keeping a journal; scape book; and write on the back of those pictures like your grandparents did. You will so much thank me especially later in life when you can look up some of those life events and tell your children and grandchildren.

Genealogy

I have learned the hard way that too much family history gets lost or forgotten the older I get. I remember when our parents and grandparents used to write stories, dates, and places on the back of pictures. I also remember when they kept all their family history written in the family bible. The bible would contain births, deaths, baptisms, stories, and all kinds of other useful information about your family history.

I didn't start doing Genealogy until my mid-fifties and I missed a lot of great information and stories because my grandmother, grandfather, and mother had already passed away. My mother was born in Holland and was a war bride. I never asked her what it was like to grow up in Holland, what her parents were like, how many brothers and sisters she had, etc. My dad didn't know too much about my mother upbringing as he met her in Germany during the end of the war. I love Genealogy and I recommend it to everyone. You might not care for it but your children and grandchildren might. I recommend that you do it sooner than later so you don't miss all of that great family history like I did.

Things I learned about marriage and love.

One of the things I learned when I graduated from high school was that a lot of my graduating class got married right out of high school. I think that a lot of them wanted to sever the ties with their parents or wanted to have kids. I don't know for sure. What I saw was a lot of divorces within a couple of years.

What I did know was that I wasn't ready for the responsibility of getting married, and I had too much playing around to do before I did. I led the singles life until I was 27, but one night when I was at my local pub drinking and playing pool a light turned on in my head that said; Jim you are ready to get married and have a family.

I was 25 years old at the time but I didn't run off and marry the first woman that was available. I just knew it was time and I was opened to the idea.

At 26 years old I was again at another bar that had live music and saw Theresa, a girl who years before had been one of my best friends girlfriend. Well as it was I had always been physically attracted to her but we had never hooked up.

Garry, her old boyfriend was getting married in a couple of weeks and I went over and asked her if she was invited to the wedding. She said she wasn't but wanted to go with me. I told her that I would have to ask Garry as I didn't know if Garry had purposely not invited her because she was an old flame. He said absolutely and wow, our first date was to Garry's wedding.

We dated for about a year and I asked Theresa to marry me and she said yes. I was deeply in love with her and we had a great marriage for 12 ½ years. We have two great sons together: Chad and Ryan. We had our ups and downs like any marriage but at the end of our marriage Theresa had that 7 year itch thing and just wanted to go out and party. I don't think she would mind me mentioning this as she told me years later that that was why she divorced me.

I had taken the divorce very hard. I am old fashion when it comes to marriage and vows. I believe in marriage is for a lifetime and I swore on my vows for better or worse; in sickness and in health; etc., that I would do everything in my power to make it work.

My integrity doesn't allow me to make a <u>liar out of myself</u>. Well we got divorced and yet we are the best of friends even today. We had sworn that if it didn't work out that we would remain friends for our sake and for the sake of the kids. Well I went into a great depression for about a year. I would sit out in the driveway in a lawn chair and my great friend Mark would come across the street and sit with me and console me. He knew how hard I had taken it. He is a very positive person and helped me get through it all. I want to thank you again, Mark.

Also thanks to Mark I got into playing darts in 1983. He and I and another good friend/neighbor would play darts every night in my garage. We had a team and often we went down to Happy Valley Inn to play darts in the Saturday night draw tournament. I had lots of dart friends and everyone liked me and saw how sad I was because of my divorce to Theresa.

One of the girls down there Karen wanted to set me up on a blind date and I said ok. She said she worked with a woman at the Stardust Hotel that was single and attractive and would ask her to come to darts the following Saturday night.

I said ok and I showed up at Happy Valley at my usual time of 7p.m. and she never showed. I was disappointed and Karen got the story from her friend Carla that she had been out to Lake Mead all day boating and was too tired to make it. So Karen called me and explained and said she would have Carla there the next Saturday.

I said ok, but it was my turn to be the stiff. My two boys asked me if I could take them to Sam Boyd Stadium to see the Super Trucks run and I caved in and didn't show up.

Karen was pretty mad at me and said she would make one more try to get us together and after that I would be on my own. So needless to say I showed up early next Saturday. A bunch of my friends had told me that Carla had showed up the previous Saturday and they just loved her; her looks; her personality; her joy; etc.

When Karen and her husband Fred came in and introduced me to Carla I was taken back. She was so beautiful and full of life, and a smile to die for. I played in the blind draw tournament but every Moment between matches I spent with Carla.

I found out that we had so much in common. We had both gone to Catholic School. We had both grown up in Southern California. We both had been previously married and had two children. Thou hers were grown and mine weren't. We were only a month apart in age. We both loved the same music and had many of the same interests, etc.

I never believed in love at first sight but I fell in love with Carla that night. About a month after dating her and calling her every night and talking for hours, I asked her to move in with me. She accepted and we lived together for 11 months before we got married.

Now here is one of the lessons I learned. I believe all people should live with each other for at least a year prior to getting married. In that year you will find out if you can live with this person for the rest of your life. You will find out any quirky habits they might have. You will find out if they have the same philosophy about things that are important to you. You will find out if that person that you have been dating just puts on an act or if they are genuinely good, etc.

Well my marriage to Carla ended after 18 years because of a huge argument. Again I don't believe Carla would mind me talking about this because it is the truth. I didn't want to get divorced just like before because of my beliefs. But life happens for a reason and we are tested along the way. <u>I've found that the harder the test, the bigger the lesson</u>.

I believe that God tests us all of our lives to prepare us for life and the bigger or harder the test is because He knows we need it and can handle it. I learned after the divorce that I needed help getting through it all and so I found a great Therapist and he helped me understand a lot of things. *The biggest lesson I learned from this marriage and divorce was that you have to be completely honest with each other and you have to communicate very well.*

Carla and I both were not great communicators because we were both non-confrontational. We held a lot of stuff in because we were afraid it would lead to an argument. You can't take things personally when having a discussion.

Ron, my therapist made sure that we both knew that when you talk and communicate that it should be a fair fight/argument with rules. That whatever was on one of our minds and it was something that bothered that person and it should be discussed and a happy medium that both of you can live with should be the end result.

Don't marry the person you think you can live with. Marry the one you can't live without.

I believe that the only advantage to getting married young is that you will probably be grandparents sooner. You will be able to do more physical things with your children because you are able too. Other than that I think it's a big mistake to get married before you have all of the playing around out of your system. Sow your oats, safely of course, but sow them so that when you finally get married you will never cheat on your spouse.

Something about ex-wives and ex-husbands: I see so many ex-wives and ex-husbands that absolutely hate each other. They can't stand to talk about them; see them; and have got nothing but bad things to think and say about them. I am the best of friends with both of my ex-wives. In fact both Theresa and Carla are best friends now. It wasn't this way at first because I was very bitter about my first divorce, but Carla who is very wise said that I should let it go and so I did. We started inviting Theresa to Holiday get togethers and we became great friends again. I have taken them both of my ex-wives out to supper together and the waiter will say, "Boy, how do you rate with two such beautiful women?" I laugh and tell him that they are my ex-wives and he can't believe it. He will say, "That's great."

About love: Love to me is so special. With both of my ex-wives I loved them not only physically but also for what was in their hearts. My wives were always my best friend.

When I looked at Theresa or Carla my heart seemed to skip a beat. In my eyes there were the most beautiful women in the world.

Now women, you may not know it but men look at other women and comment on them sometimes. But if you are truly in love with somebody then you will never cross that line of cheating on them. Its human nature to look at beautiful women and if you're a woman, then handsome/cute men. But you have to have enough confidence in yourself and your marriage to not be jealous. And it goes both ways. Women can look and comment about a cute or good looking actor on TV or person out if public, but never cross that line of actually cheating on your spouse.

Something else too women: I've personally always liked to hold hands. Even now days it makes me feel like a kid again. But when a woman takes your arm, you all of a sudden hold your head high and strut along with this pride in your heart. You know you have a beautiful woman holding on to you and you just want to show her off.

Everyone needs to have Agape Love for their spouses. Agape Love is what a pet give to you. In the dictionary Agape Love is selfless love of another person with expectations of a sexual nature.

I've learned that most of us don't do the same things that we did when we were dating and won the love of the one we love. We would talk for hours on the phone; take breath mints; send flowers and love cards; pull out the chair or open the door you your female dates, etc.

Why after we are married do we quit doing those things? Where's the romance? Don't ever stop doing the things that made that special person fall in love with you. And remember men: <u>Happy Wife, Happy Life!</u>

Here's an idea I wished I had learned when my Mom was alive. On Your birthday, send her flowers for giving birth to you. I know there is Mother's Day, but she was the one that carried you around and took care of you. It is she that should get a gift from you!

I learned late in life that a husband and a Wife should have their own checking and savings accounts. I took that away from my second Wife Carla and later found out that she felt like she lost her independence.

She had been a single mother for years and used to having her own account and when we combined our accounts and I started paying the bills, she felt like she couldn't spend any money, (even thou she had income), and lost her independence. I believe that one person should pay the bills but that you should do it together so that you both know where your money is going. This would be very informative, a good check and balance system, and is fair to both people.

Credit Cards: I believe Credit Cards should be called _Emergency Cards_. The old saying that you should never charge more than you can pay back in 30 days is so true, but emergencies do come up. You can't rent a car without one; you can't reserve a room at a Hotel without one; you can't pre-buy an airplane flight online without one.

Of course if you follow the new theory of putting away 1 years-worth of income away for emergencies or loss of a job then you won't need that Emergency Card to replace a broken appliance or what not. I believe that the credit card companies give too much credit sometimes. Each situation is different and personal. Usually now days you could get away with $750 to $1000 limit, but $10,000 is prohibitive.

Did you know that if you just make the minimum payment on a credit card that it takes 16 years to pay it off!

Three Things that Really Upset Me

I've learned throughout the years that there are only 3 things that will really piss me off.

The first is: Do not ever lie to me for any reason. Tell me truth even if it is hurtful to you or me.

The second is: Do not ever disrespect me. I especially do not allow this from any of my children to either me or their mother.

The third is: Do not ever ever steal from me. If you do I will hire a battalion of lawyers and put the handcuffs on myself. And I will ensure that you will pay for your crime with everything cent I got. This is not vindictive. This is one of the 10 Commandments.

Retirement and Care Takers

What I have learned about Retirement: This is probably the biggest lesson I have learned. I became a care giver to my dad in October of 2012. I love my dad so dearly. He is 87 years old and has so many physical problems that there are too many to list. But I have learned more about my dad since he now lives with me that during my whole time of growing up as his oldest son.

My dad retired at age 53. His second Wife Mary told him it was ok for him to do so. He cited that he retired because of exhaustion. Well the biggest problem my dad had when he retired is that he retired from life. He like so many people couldn't wait to retire.

But he thought that when you retire that life is over. He didn't do anything but fish, (which is good), read, and watch TV. For the last 34 years he didn't and now he can't do anything else. He can't even fish anymore. I have told him the old saying that, (you use it, or you lose it.)" Everyone has to realize that if you don't take care of yourself physically you will after time lose the ability to walk; open a bottle of water; open a soda; and everything else that you took for granted for years.

Here is the bottom line for everyone that wants to retire. Yes, retire when you are financially able to. But do not under any circumstance, Retire from Life. Take those vacations you didn't have time for. Do those projects around the house you didn't have time for. Do all the things on your Bucket List. But when you have done all those things then make a plan for the rest of your remaining years.

Make short term plans; medium term plans; and long term plans. Do not stop exercising and just sit on the couch, read and watch TV. Find a hobby that involves some sort of physical movement. They say that if you just sit around and don't do anything that you will lose about 10% of you muscle mass per year. I don't know if I agree with the 10% thing but I do know that if anyone has ever broken an arm or a leg and had to wear a cast for an extended period of time that you will see just how much muscle a person can lose in a very short period of time when the cast comes off.

Your life isn't supposed to end when you retire. I believe it's just a New Chapter in Your Life. There is so much more that you can do. People are living so much longer these days than they did 100 years ago. The body was actually made to last about 120 years. Make that list of goals and include things that you are physically able to do right now. My Uncle Bruce sent me a story about a 98 year old man that plays golf. He was a professional when he was young and then a golf instructor. He has shot better than his age more than 3000 times. For those of you that know the game of golf, you know how hard this feat is. At 98 years old he still walks 2 ½ miles every day. So no excuses people, Ha! Anything is possible.

Until I was a caretaker I didn't know how hard it would be or time consuming. My dad is a handful to take care of. My ex-wife Carla developed M.S. in 1994, and I had to give her shots, and do various things related to the disease. I want to tell everyone that reads this book how much I appreciate what they have to do. A lot of people have it worse that I do in that they have to take care of parents and children that have diseases, are crippled, mentally challenged, etc. The old saying, "you come into this world as a baby, and you go out of this world as a baby is so true". I feel so good about taking care of my dad. I feel like I am paying him back for all of his sacrifices and for raising me for 18 years.

Volunteering when you Retire

I had to volunteer at a place called Opportunity Village. I say had to because I was unemployed and Nevada Job Connect which is the unemployment office wanted to evaluate me.

Opportunity Village is a place where people of all ages over 18 years old and that are mentally challenged can work. These people are called Special People by the employees.

The first day I worked there I was taken back by all the Special People and their handicaps, and I felt very sad for them. But I soon learned that they are the most joyest of people. They love to work.

They can't wait for Fridays, not because they want the weekend off, but because that's payday. They earn very little money, but to them it is a lot. And they are so proud of their little checks. They all wanted me to see their checks and were like I said, they were so proud.

I learned that everybody should take a turn at volunteering. It gave me so much pleasure and I want everyone to try it and feel the pleasure I felt. It makes you especially feel how lucky you are to be in good health and it's very rewarding.

There are so many places you can volunteer: the VA, Vet Hospitals. Pet shelters walking dogs, soup kitchens to name just a few.

Manners and Politeness

I was raised to be polite by my parents and the Catholic Nuns. I have remained that way all of my life, but I see and meet so many people that are just rude; lacking of manners and politeness; and lacking respect. Have you ever noticed how polite the Japanese are? And their children are so polite and respectful. If you have ever watched the Little League World Series you will see the Japanese kids bow or salute the umpires; they never argue; and they have the greatest of respect for the game, etc.

Both of my boys Chad and Ryan enlisted in the Service. Chad went into the Air Force and just celebrated his 14th year, and Ryan did his turn in the Army. But what I remember most is their Basic Training Graduations. They were so respectful to everyone. It was, "Yes and no ma'am, and yes and no sir," to everyone they came in contact with".

I am very proud of them for protecting our freedom and serving our Country. They are both very polite good citizens. I have learned that the Armed Forces will teach you respect, politeness, manners, and you will come out of Basic Training in the best shape of your life.

Here's an idea. How about if we send out children to Basic Training when they are 16 years old for 6 weeks during summer vacation?

There is an old grade school song that has stuck with me, it goes something like this: Thank you, may I, excuse me, please. These are the words we say with ease.

Positive and Negative Attitudes

Some people don't seem to ever be happy. They frown; they don't smile; they are mad at something all the time; or they seem to be happy being sad.

I touched on this earlier when I was talking about affirmations and programing your mind to think positive. Only you and you alone have the power to program yourself to think and act positively.

It is proven that Positive and Negative thoughts are controlled by different parts of the mind. And that Negative thoughts take up more space in the brain than Positive thoughts do. You have to control your Negative thoughts by catching them and converting them to a Positive thought.

There are so many positive things or victories in your life. You just have to remember them. It could be when you graduated from High School: maybe when you got your first promotion on your job: maybe when you learned to drive or got your first vehicle: maybe when you got married or had your first child. Whatever your victory was is a Positive Thought.

I've learned to recognize when I am not being positive and to convert those negative thoughts into positive thoughts. You will find that you will have a much more happy life if you can do this.

One thing that will help you keep a Positive Attitude is to say Affirmations every day. Pick out several affirmations and repeat them over and over and end them with: In the name of Jesus Christ. I do my every single day when I walk my dog. I have several that I repeat over and over. I am living proof that they work. I am totally amazed by how well they work.

Another way of doing affirmations is to write or print them on a piece of paper out and hang them on your bathroom mirror and say them every morning when you shaving; doing your hair; brushing your teeth; etc.

Have you ever noticed that when you ask certain people how they are you get some really negative responses? For Example: How are you Bill? Not worth a damn; Not so good; Just alright; I'm fair; Good, etc. Well even, "Good" is just an average response. Try these: I'm great: I'm fabulous; I'm terrific; I'm blessed; I'm wonderful! I've learned that when you enthusiastically give a response like this it brings a smile to people's faces and it also programs you to live a great day.

Every thought you have is either negative or positive. What a remarkable statement!

Think about that for a second. Every word you SAY or THINK is either NEGATIVE or POSITIVE!

Which are you doing at all times?

You can tell a lot about how a person wears his/her face and carries their body. I'm talking again about body language; eyes; smiles; and posture. You can tell a lot about a person just by their eyes. There are soft eyes; glaring eyes; scared eyes; happy eyes; shocked eyes; and eyes that reveal kindness of the heart, etc. There are people that have permanent upside down creases in their face because they never smile. There are people that always smile and it shows. But the best smile in my opinion is the full teeth smile. Next time you meet someone new look them over and see what I mean, but don't prejudge them because you don't know what kind of life they've led.

Today you are going to learn how to make "What you want" match your thoughts!

Whatever you are thinking and feeling today is creating your future.

Good Feelings	Bad Feelings
Love	Resentment
Gratitude	Guilt
Joy	Depression
Passion	Fear
Happiness	Hate
Enlightment	Revenge/Anger

Some More Words of Wisdom

1. The worst thing about being lied to is simply knowing you weren't worth the truth.
2. The truth may hurt for a little while, but a lie hurts forever.
3. Don't be easy to get because you'll be easy to forget.
4. People come and go; you just gotta know who are those worth having, worth waiting for, and those worth dumping.
5. Strangers can become best friends just as easy as best friends can become strangers.
6. If you feel you can't live without them, just remember you survived long before them.
7. Being in a relationship is not about kissing, dates, or showing off. It's about being with the person who makes you happy.
8. Do what makes you happy, with the one who makes you smile, laugh as much as you breathe, and love as long as you live.
9. When you truly love someone you don't judge them by their past, you accept it and leave it there.
10. Life is too short to wake up with regrets . . . So love the people who treat you right . . . stop stressing the ones who don't.
11. Just because someone left, doesn't mean your happiness is gone. Happiness doesn't depend on anybody but ourselves.
12. Never hate people who are jealous of you, but respect their jealousy. They're people who think that you're better than them.

13. Don't waste your time giving someone a second chance, when there's someone better out there waiting for their first.
14. Its sweet when someone remembers every little detail about you, not because you keep reminding them, but because they pay attention.
15. You can tell as much about a person based on what they say about others, as you can based on what others say about them.
16. Sometimes you have to care less, in order to see if they'll care more.
17. One of the simplest ways to stay happy is to let go of the things that make you sad.
18. There are two sure ways to know what a person is really like. One is the way that person treats a waiter or a waitress, and the other is to play a round of golf with them. Jim Imes
19. Sometimes you have to let things go, so there's room for better things to come into your life
20. Never be afraid to speak your mind we all have one for a reason.
21. People are like a fine wine. They get better with age! Jim Imes
22. Patience with others is love, patience with yourself is hope, and patience with God is faith.
23. Life is too short to wake up with regrets, so love the people who treat you right and forget the ones who don't.
24. You can't control anyone's actions but your own, so be a good person and eventually good will come to you.
25. Nobody can go back and start a new beginning, but anyone can start today and make a new ending.

26. Without humor life is boring. Without love life is hopeless. Without friends like your life is impossible.
27. You'll never really understand a person until you consider things from their point of view.
28. One of the biggest mistakes you can make is to drift away from someone you once had the time of your life with.
29. Being there for people because you know what it's like to have no one there for you.
30. If you still talk about it you still care about it.
31. The longer you hide your feelings for someone, the more you fall for them.
32. It takes knowledge to stop doing something wrong, but it takes wisdom to keep doing something right.
33. An argument is to find out who is right. A discussion it to find out what is right.
34. When you feel you're at your lowest point, just stay positive and know that things can only go up from there.
35. When you really matter to someone, that person will always make time for you. No excuses. No lies. No broken promises.
36. You don't need someone to complete you. You only need someone to accept you completely.
37. Forget what has hurt you in the past, but never forget what it has taught you.
38. Yesterday is history. Tomorrow is a mystery. Today is a gift. That's why it's called the present.
39. Most people spend their time trying to find someone to sleep with instead of finding someone worth waking up to . . .
40. In a relationship, the one who loves more is the one who hurts most.

41. Its funny how you can do nice things for people all the time and they never notice. But once you make one mistake, it's never forgotten.
42. Words don't have power to hurt you, unless that person means a lot to you . . .
43. Sometimes you gotta accept the fact that certain things will NEVER go back to how they use to be.
44. There are three types of people in this world: Ones you wish you had, Ones you will always have, and ones you once had.
45. Be Good To Yourself Because the Longest Relationship You Will Ever Have In Life Is With Yourself.
46. If you lose my trust, you're not getting it back unless you work for it. Even then, it probably won't be the same.
47. A mistake is only a mistake if you don't learn from it.
48. You don't really need someone to complete you. You only need someone to accept you completely.
49. I've made lots of mistakes in my past . . . but if you judge me on what I did in my past, then you have no reason being in my future.
50. Be who you are and don't apologize. Life is too short to do it any other way.
51. Instead of spending your energy on hating your enemies, use it to love your friends a little harder.
52. Faith is taking that first step, even when you don't see the light at the end of the tunnel. Jim Imes
53. People will hate you, rate you, shake you, and break you. But how strong you stand is what makes you.
54. Don't forget to pray tonight because God didn't forget to wake you up this morning.

55. Remember those who helped you up, and never forget those that put you down.
56. Don't be what people want you to be. Be yourself and find someone who truly loves you for what and who you are.
57. Your choices, your actions, your life, live it your way with no regrets.
58. True love is when you care about their happiness more than your own.
59. A man once approached Socrates and asked the great teacher to help him learn. The master took his would be student into a river and pushed him under water, and held him there! Struggling back to the surface, the young man shouted, "Why did you do that?" and Socrates replied. "When you want to learn as much as you wanted to breathe, you will."
60. I would rather live my life as if there is a God; and die to find out there isn't; than live my life as if there isn't; and die to find out there is. How true!

Some More Good Thoughts about What I Have Learned.

Common Sense

Beware of the doctor who prescribes surgery for a common cold.

When people today complain about people today, aren't they complaining about themselves?

Take it to your brain before you take it to your boss.

Problem solving and positive change have something in common . . . they both begin with me. And each of us is me!

Rules are meant to be followed. If they weren't, they'd be called "suggestions".

To be empathetic is to be understanding and considerate . . . to attempt to see things from another person's point of view.

Instead of always looking for what's wrong and trying to fix it, focus once in a while on finding what's right and celebrate it!

Some people hear but don't listen. Listening is a skill that must be developed.

Quality comes from a quality culture . . . quality comes from people. It happens one day at a time, one person at a time, and one behavior at a time. What if your quality program showed up for work, but your people didn't? It's not the management of quality that matters most . . . it's the quality of *management!*

A good employee is one who adds value and gets results.

People who think ignorance is bliss are probably very blissful.

Look for and create opportunities to learn, grow, and continually improve.

If punishment really works, then why do we have "repeat offenders"?

The best way to break a bad habit is to drop it!

If you ignore other people, does that make you an *ignoramus*?

Brains are like closets. Over time, they become filled with things we no longer use, (bad programs, bad values, etc.) . . . Things that no longer apply or fit. Every once in a while they need to be cleaned out!

If you only work on you weaknesses, you just might end up with a business filled with very strong weaknesses!

Have the courage to bet on your ideas, to take the calculated risk, and then to act.

Recognition is another word for reward.

The tide of opportunity comes to everyone. Be ready.

Recognize and accept that change will take place. Integrity can only be one thing and that is <u>consistency</u>. You cannot tell the truth 90% of the time and lie 10% of the time and claim to be a person of Integrity. It doesn't work that way. Jim Imes

There are too many people in this world that use their power and money to hurt people. Thru some defect in their values and morals they derive pleasure from this. Trust your instinct and don't work or associate with these people. Work and associate with the pure of heart that lift you up. Jim Imes

Work is like a ten-speed bicycle. Most of us have gears we never use.—Jim Imes

The real measure of your wealth is how much you'd be worth if you lost all of your money.

People don't care how much you know . . . Until they know how much you care.

"How many times have you taken action on things you don't desire, imagine if you took action on the things you do."

It takes a long time to make it to the top, but one short step to end up on the bottom.

Our lives are not determined by what happens to us but by how we react to what happens, not by what life brings to us, but by the attitude we bring to life. A positive attitude causes a chain reaction of positive thoughts, events, and outcomes. It is a catalyst, a spark that creates extraordinary results.

Some Sayings and Advice about Worry
Why worry?

There are only two things to worry about: Either you are well or you are sick. If you are well, then there is nothing to worry about:

But if you are sick, there are only two things to worry about:

Whether you will get well, or whether you will die.

If you get well, there is nothing to worry about; but if you die, there are only two things to worry about: Whether you go to heaven or hell.

If you go to heaven, there is nothing to worry about: And if you go to hell you'll be so busy shaking hands with old friends, you won't have time to worry. If you worry, will it change the future?

Why worry, it will probably never happen.

Worry: always ask yourself if you can do anything about it right now. If you can then do it. If you cannot, then write it down and don't give it another thought until a time when you can.

If you spend as much time doing the things you worry about as you do worrying about doing them, you wouldn't have anything to worry about.

Do not worry about whether or not the sun will rise. Be prepared to enjoy it.

Worry is interest paid in advance.

It has been found that the things that people worry about in 95% of the cases, never come to pass.

Live in the now!

We must use time as a tool, not as a couch.

Only fools live in the past, or carry envy into the future.

Don't let yesterday use up today. The future is purchased by the present.

You will never demonstrate money while you are pathetic and live in the past. Live fully in the now.

Learn from the past, plan for the future, and live in the present.

Chapter 5

THE TIME CHAPTER

Time is a Gift

A successful manager of time is willing to do that which the unsuccessful manager of time is not willing to do.

Until you value yourself, you will not value your time. Until you value your time, you will not do anything with it.

Do you love life? Then do not squander time, for that's the stuff life is made of.

What I do today is important because I am paying for it with a day of my life. What I accomplish must be worthwhile because the price is very high.

Procrastination is the thief of time.

Nothing is the world is more precious than time. All the money in the world cannot buy back even one second of time.

One thing you can't recycle is wasted time.

The wasting of time is the most costly of all expenses.

(Time) invest it so as to get from it the utmost in health, happiness, and success! The clock is running.

They say it takes a minute to find a special person; an hour to appreciate them; a day to love them; but then an entire life to forget them.

Take the time to live and love.

Chapter 6

FUNNY OBSERVATIONS AND GREAT TRUTHS

1) When I die I want to die like my grandfather—who died peacefully in his sleep. Not screaming like all the passengers in his car."
2) Advice for the day: If you have a lot of tension and you get a headache, do what it says on the aspirin bottle: "Take two aspirin" and "Keep away from children."

GREAT TRUTHS THAT LITTLE CHILDREN HAVE LEARNED:

1) No matter how hard you try, you can't baptize cats.
2) When your Mom is mad at your Dad, don't let her brush your hair.
3) If your sister hits you, don't hit her back. They always catch the second person.
4) Never ask your 3-year old brother to hold a tomato.
5) You can't trust dogs to watch your food.
6) Don't sneeze when someone is cutting your hair.
7) Never hold a Dust-Buster and a cat at the same time.
8) You can't hide a piece of broccoli in a glass of milk.

9) Don't wear polka-dot underwear under white shorts.
10) The best place to be when you're sad is Grandpa's lap.

GREAT TRUTHS THAT ADULTS HAVE LEARNED:

1) Raising teenagers is like nailing Jell-O to a tree.
2) Wrinkles don't hurt.
3) Families are like fudge . . . mostly sweet, with a few nuts.
4) Today's mighty oak is just yesterday's nut that held its ground.
5) Laughing is good exercise. It's like jogging on the inside.
6) Middle age is when you choose your cereal for the fiber, not the joy.
7) Raising children is like getting pecked all your life by a chicken.

GREAT TRUTHS ABOUT GROWING OLD:

1) Growing old is mandatory; growing up is optional.
2) Forget the health food. I need all the preservatives I can get.
3) When you fall down, you wonder what else you can do while you're down there.
4) You're getting old when you get the same sensation from a rocking chair that you once got from a roller coaster.
5) Its frustrating when you know all the answers but nobody bothers to ask you the questions.

6) Time may be a great healer, but it's a lousy beautician.
7) Wisdom comes with age, but sometimes age comes alone.

THE FOUR STAGES OF LIFE:

1) You believe in Santa Claus.
2) You don't believe in Santa Claus.
3) You are Santa Claus.
4) You look like Santa Claus.

SUCCESS:

At age 4 successes is not peeing in your pants.
At age 12 successes is having a friend.
At age 16 success is having a driver's license.
At age 20 success is having sex.
At age 35 success is having money.
At age 50 success is having money.
At age 60 success is having sex.
At age 70 success is having a driver's license.
At age 75 success is having friends.
At age 80 success is not peeing in your pants.

The Creative Process

♦ Ask: Let the universe know what you want. Write it down.
♦ Believe your wish is my command.
♦ Replace doubt with faith.

◆ Receive: feel good—be happy for it to happen—
This is a feeling universe.

◆ Do whatever it takes to manifest the
feelings—touch it, drive it, look at homes, paste
on the wall, actions may be required, but you
must like it.

The universe likes speed. Don't delay. Don't second
guess. Don't doubt. When the opportunity is there; when
the intuitive is there; then ask.

Visualize—Then you Materialize—Feel It

◆ Decide what you want
◆ Believe you can have it
◆ Believe you deserve it
◆ Believe it's possible for you
◆ Close your eyes every day and visualize

Accidental Discoveries

1. LSD
    Swiss chemist Albert Hofmann was trying to come
    up with a chemical to induce childbirth. Instead he
    developed lysergic acid diethylamide, or LSD. After
    he tried a bigger dose he made another discovery!
    A bad acid trip.

2. X-ray
    Several 19th-century scientists played around with
    the penetrating rays emitted when electrons struck

a metal target. But the x-ray wasn't discovered until 1895, when Wilhelm Röntgen tried sticking various objects in front of the radiation and saw the bones of his hand projected on a wall.

3. Penicillin
   Scottish scientist Alexander Fleming was researching the flu in 1928 when he noticed that a blue-green mold had infected one of his petri dishes and killed the staphylococcus bacteria growing in it.

4. Microwave ovens
   The microwave oven came along in the 1940s. Microwave emitters (or magnetrons), were being used to power Allied radar during WWII. It was after a magnetron melted a candy bar in Raytheon that engineer Percy Spencer's pocket that the common use for a microwave emitter was realized.

5. Potato chips
   Chef George Crum concocted the perfect sandwich complement in 1853 when to spite a customer who complained that his fries were cut too thick—he sliced a potato paper thin and fried it to a crisp.

6. Artificial sweeteners
   Speaking of botched lab jobs three leading pseudo-sugars reached human lips only because scientists forgot to wash their hands. Cyclamate (1937) and aspartame (1965) are byproducts of medical research and saccharin (1879) appeared during a project on coal tar derivatives

Chapter 7

POLITICS

Politics is the most controversial topic I believe anyone can address. I also believe it to be one of the most important because it impacts all of us as future Americas. Everything that I say about Politics is just point of view and my opinions.

Politics: I have a love hate relationship with Politics. I grew up like a lot of little boys, wanting to be President when I grew up. As I grew old enough to know and see Politics for what it really is, I changed my mind. I got very disheartened.

It has gotten so corrupt in the last 25 years. It has moved so far away from the ideals that our Founding Fathers had hoped it would be. It is driven now by Big Money; Big Companies; Special Interest Groups; and Politicians that don't represent the people anymore. They have their own agendas and the agendas of the Big Money that put them in office.

I don't believe that they all start out that way but Washington, pressure from their party, pressure from the money donations of certain groups have made them that way.

That for the most part, isn't what Americans want and is why we are not represented properly. I have always voted since I was 18 years old. My dad taught me that it is my civic duty to vote. I believe that people that live in American that don't vote have no business talking or expressing politics. To complain about the government and then not vote, doesn't add up.

I have been a Democrat; Independent; and a Republican. I have always voted for the person running according to my values and beliefs and their value and beliefs. I have always voted for the person. Not along Political lines just because I registered with one party or another. I personally am a Moderate Conservative at this point in my life.

Am I the only one that thinks when you are running for Office of Presidency that the candidates should have a Lie Detector hooked up to them when they Debate? I can see it now. The hard questions put to them on Television with the needle jumping all over the place when they lie. And of course we could then tell when they are telling the truth.

There are other ways that politics has gotten so dirty. The personal attacks on both Television and on the Campaign Trail; the personal attacks on both daytime talk shows and late night shows; the news media; famous political newspapers; not to mention the personal attacks to their families.

And the famous people that endorse certain candidates on Television is just wrong. I'm not saying they shouldn't favor one candidate over another, but when one famous person can sway over a million people to vote along with their personal chosen candidate, that's wrong.

That means that one famous persons vote isn't just one vote but a million, or 500000, or 100000. There is a show that I love to watch when it's not voting time. That show has 4 Liberals and 1 Conservative on it. And every 4 years during the Presidential election it is so one sided that it's not fair. And this show influences millions of viewers too.

The late night talk and comedy shows make fun at certain candidates to the point of dragging them down to their level in my opinion. Where is their integrity? Where is the television stations integrity? I think that all major Television stations; newspapers; magazines; etc. should present each candidate with an unbiased view. To present us with the truth so we can make the best choice. Of course it's their right not to but we the people deserve it. We are voting for the most powerful person in the world to run our country. Should we expect anything less?

I wish these Hollywood leftist Liberals would quit spending our hard earned tax dollars and if they are so bent on helping every living creature and being in the United States they could adopt them. Most of the biggest influencers are fairly rich. Some are millionaires or billionaires. Depending on how much money they have they could adopt 25 families to a 1000 and support them themselves; just an idea!

If it wasn't for any of these people living in America, what would their chances of becoming rich and famous in the first place? If they were born and lived in anything but a free nation, they probably would be a laborer; dish washer; teacher; waiter; farmer; or some other trade. No but they live in the Land of the Free and kudos to them for making it to the level they are at.

When you ask 100 Americans what kind of country are we? You will get 90% of them saying that we are a Democracy and this would be wrong. Our Founding Fathers made it very clear that we are a Republic. By definition, a republic is a representative form of government that is ruled according to a charter, or constitution, and a democracy is a government that is ruled according to the will of the majority.

Although these forms of government are often confused, they are quite different. The main difference between a republic and a democracy is the charter or constitution that limits power in a republic, often to protect the individual's rights against the desires of the majority. We should look at history and know that Democracy just doesn't work. The longest any Democracy has ever lasted is about 300 years. Other governments that haven't worked for any extended amount of time are: Dictatorships, Marxism, Communism, and Socialism.

The Founding Father knew this. It didn't work for the ancient Greeks or Romans. The simple truth is that people will vote themselves all kinds of benefits with no regard to how it's going to be paid for. When the benefits exceed the amount of money that the American Tax Payers can pay then Democracy fails.

The Pledge of Allegiance: *I pledge allegiance to the Flag of the United States of America, and to the Republic for which it stands, one Nation under God, indivisible, with liberty and justice for all.*

I will say that the Founding Fathers wanted the Government to be small. They wanted this for so many reasons but for the most part they knew the Government would be terrible at running what should be private programs and that except for providing a strong military they should keep their hands out of it because they would have to be funded by the tax payers.

They also knew that a government to big could take your freedoms away. Now look at all the programs that the Government has implemented like Social Security; Welfare; the Post Office; etc. Every single one of them loses money; is mismanaged; is borrowing or shifting money; etc. (did you know that NASA borrowed millions from Social Security and never paid it back?). Look at how profitable private industries are like: Fed-Ex, DHL, UPS, Insurance Companies, etc. And now we are going to have the Government run our Healthcare System.

Where and when is it going to stop? ***The definition of Insanity is doing the same thing over and over, and expecting different results***. We Americans keep letting our Government make the same mistakes over and over.

What if History didn't play out the way it did?

What if England didn't allow the Colonists to have guns for the purpose of hunting? We would never have been able to form a militia and the Revolutionary War would have never happened. We would still be under the rule of England.

What if there was no Civil War? Blacks would still be slaves.

What if the Civil war was a draw? There would be a Northern Nation and a Southern Nation. What would that of meant to our future.

What if we lost the Mexican American War? What would that mean that mean? Would Texas, Arizona, and California all have become part of Mexico?

What if we didn't win the war with Germany and Japan? Would that mean that Germany would rule the Eastern half of the United States and Japan would rule the Western part of the United States? Etc.

Gives you something to think about, doesn't it? That is why history is so important to learn. Just like you don't want your kids to suffer the same mistakes that you made, you shouldn't want America to make the same mistake that other nations throughout time have made.

Here is what is going to happen if we as a nation keep going in the direction we have taken the last 40 years give or take.

We currently have the Halves and the Halve Nots. You could call them the working people and the non-working people. You have the 2 major parties, Democrats and Republicans. You have illegals living here and voting too. You have 16% of the population that works for the government. Knowing all of this, this is what is coming up very soon in our future. The 16% that are working for the government are always going to vote to insure they have a job, which more than likely means voting for the Democratic candidate. There are somewhere between 12 and 20 million illegal aliens in the U.S., (nobody knows for sure how many).

There are a certain amount of voters that are going to vote along party lines no matter who the candidate is. There is a shrinking number of Halves that either can't find work or got on a program in which the government supports them.

There are spouses of the employed government workers that are going to vote to help protect their spouse's jobs, (That would now bring 16% to perhaps 32%). This now puts us way over 50% of the voters and that means we can never go back to elections where we can vote in the better candidate.

This also means we are not a Republic anymore and are now a Socialist Country. And with the added expenses the new healthcare program brings our credit rating is going to go down again.

Combine all these things and eventually not only will we fail like Rome and Greece did, but "We the People" will not be running the country anymore. This is the number one reason our Fore Fathers created a Republic instead of a Democracy, along with instituting the 2nd Amendment. We will end up powerless and broke.

No one including China will lend us money to support the overwhelming amount or prohibitive programs and debt that we have instituted over the years. We won't be able to afford our Military, (that's already happening), etc. etc. etc.

Examples of more Economic Sense

1. Nothing in our material world can come from nowhere or go nowhere, nor can it be free: everything in our economic life has a source, a destination, and a cost that must be paid.
2. Government is never a source of goods. The people produce everything produced, and everything that government gives to the people, it must first take from the people.
3. The only valuable money that government has to spend is that money taxed or borrowed out of the people's earnings. When government decides to spend more than it has thus received, that extra-unearned money is created out of thin air, through the banks, and when spent, takes on value only by reducing the value of all money, savings, and insurance.
4. In our modern exchange economy, all payroll and employment come from customers, and the only worthwhile job security is customer security; if there

are no customers, there can be no payroll and no jobs.

5. Customer security can be achieved by the worker, only when he/she cooperates with management in doing the things that win and hold customers. Job security, therefore, is a partnership problem that can solve only in a spirit of understanding and cooperation.

6. Because wages are the principal cost of everything, widespread wage increases, without corresponding increases in production, simply increase the cost of everybody's living.

7. The greatest good for the greatest number means, in its material sense, the greatest goods for the greatest number which, in turn, means the greatest productivity per worker.

8. All productivity is based on three factors: 1) natural resources, whose form, place and condition are changed by the expenditure of, 2) human energy (both muscular and mental), with the aid of, 3) tools.

9. Tools are the only one of these three factors that man can increase without limit, and tools come into being in a free society only when there is a reward for the temporary self-denial that people must practice in order to channel part of the earnings away from purchases that produce immediate comfort and pleasure, and into new tools of production. Proper payment for the use of tools is essential to their creation.

10. The productivity of the tools-that is, the efficiency of the human energy applied in connection with

their use-has always been highest in a competitive society in which the economic decisions are made by millions of progress-seeking individuals, rather than in a state-planned society in which those decisions are made by a handful of all-powerful people, regardless of how ill-meaning, unselfish, sincere and intelligent those people may be.

"The Constitution is not an instrument for the government to restrain the people; it is an instrument for the people to restrain the government."

I could go on for hours and hours because I am very passionate about our country, history, and politics, but I won't. I am going to post some of the more popular quotes from our famous presidents for you to enjoy and hopefully absorb.

Famous Presidential Quotes

George Washington (1789-1797)

"To be prepared for war is one of the most effectual means of preserving peace."

"Few men have virtue to withstand the highest bidder". "Special Interests Groups which cause Pork."

"Liberty, when it begins to take root, is a plant of rapid growth."

John Adams (1707-1801)

"I pray Heaven to bestow the best of blessing on this house (the White House) and on all that shall hereafter inhabit it. May none but honest and wise men ever rule under this roof!"

"The happiness of society is the end of government."

Thomas Jefferson (1801-1809)

"The price of freedom is eternal vigilance."

"When government fears the people, there is liberty. When the people fear the government, there is tyranny."

Andrew Jackson (1829-1837)

"Internal improvement and the diffusion of knowledge, so far as they can be promoted by the constitutional acts of the Federal Government, are of high importance."

"One man with courage is a majority."

"That government is best which governs the least, because its people discipline themselves."